on MOUNT HOOD

on MOUNT HOOD

A Biography of Oregon's Perilous Peak

JON BELL

SASQUATCH BOOKS
SEATTLE

Printed in the United States of America
Published by Sasquatch Books
Distributed by PGW/Perseus
17 16 15 14 13 12 11   9 8 7 6 5 4 3 2 1

Cover photograph: © James Hearn / Dreamstime.com
Cover and interior design: Anna Goldstein
Map: Liza Brice-Dahmen / map created using TOPO! software © 2010
    National Geographic Maps / TOPO maps produced by the U.S Geological
    Survey
Interior composition: Anna Goldstein
Back cover photograph and all interior photographs by Jon Bell except
    page ix, Mark Malaska; pages 8 and 105, Trin Yuthasastrakosol;
    pages 53 and 183, Amy Bell; and page 94, Scott Baker.

Library of Congress Cataloging-in-Publication Data
Bell, Jon.
   On Mount Hood : a biography of Oregon's perilous peak / Jon Bell.
      p. cm.
   Includes bibliographical references and index.
   ISBN-13: 978-1-57061-692-1 (alk. paper)
   ISBN-10: 1-57061-692-2 (alk. paper)
   1. Hood, Mount (Or.)--History. 2. Natural history--Oregon--Hood,
   Mount. 3. Hood, Mount (Or.)--Description and travel. 4. Bell, Jon--
   Travel--Oregon--Hood, Mount. 5. Mountaineering--Oregon--
   Mount--History. 6. Mountaineers--Oregon--Hood, Mount--Biography.
   7. Hood, Mount (Or.)--Biography. I. Title.
   F882.H85B45 2010
   979.5'61--dc22
                              2010049932

Sasquatch Books
119 South Main Street, Suite 400
Seattle, WA 98104
(206) 467-4300
www.sasquatchbooks.com
custserv@sasquatchbooks.com

For Amy, of course.

CONTENTS

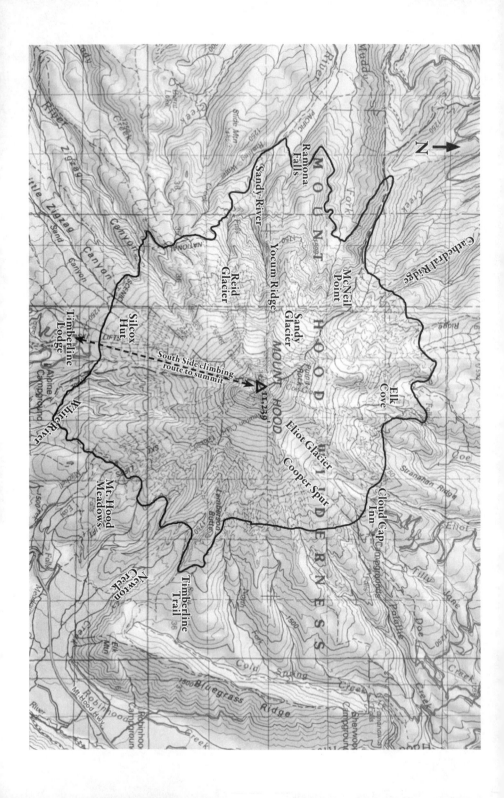

INTRODUCTION

Oh you feel and you taste it
And you want to go higher, so what do you do
And so you peek into the mountain
Where your desire goes

—ERIKA WENNERSTROM, "The Mountain"

OUNT HOOD'S IS NOT A STORY that I intentionally set
out to know. It's one that instead has slowly been built for
me since the very first time I laid eyes on the mountain. Hailing
from far away, like so many modern-day Oregonians, I'd never
seen the mountain except in pictures until I sped into Portland
along the Terwilliger Curves of I-5 one memorable autumn day
in 1997. All of my belongings were in one car, all of Amy's, my
future wife, in another. We were transplanting ourselves into the
next chapter of a life that had already taken us from a spring break
meeting in Florida to a summer in northern Michigan, through

the Rocky Mountains of Colorado and to the snow-draped Sierra Nevada on the shores of Lake Tahoe, California.

By the time we decided to pack up and explore Oregon, I'd already learned to love the mountains of the West. But seeing a snowy Mount Hood on the horizon for the first time was truly entrancing—a sight that brands your perception, marks your memory, nearly sends you careening off the road. Were someone to drive through Portland along I-5 on a cloudy winter day, they'd never know the beautiful peak they were missing. Drive through on a lucky fall afternoon, however, when the snow up on Hood is new and blinding white, and they'll never forget it.

Since that wild October day—I remember crossing the Burnside Bridge in downtown Portland during rush-hour traffic, Amy keeping me in her sights from behind thanks to the bright red, seventeen-foot canoe on the roof of my car—I have explored the mountain, gotten to know it, lived with it, and learned its story throughout all my days here. When you live so close to something so enchanting, it's hard not to. I've headed to the mountain for solitude and escape, to refresh and purge for another go at life in the workaday world. I've watched with excitement as friends and family from across the country have laid their eyes on it for the very first time. I've made friends on its shoulders at 10,000 feet, been humbled by centuries-old trees that rise in its shadow, traded tales with complete strangers about the common ground we've shared on Mount Hood.

Whether hiking or climbing or skiing or camping on it, gazing longingly at it from an office window, sipping a pale ale with its countenance on the label, enduring the rain it wrings from the air, following a story about climbers lost on it or massive trees about to be cut on it, Hood has a story that inevitably becomes a part of your own. The mountain's presence is undeniable and iconic, always there, whether you can see it or not. It is a paragon of alpine beauty, but also in its entirety much more than that. Mount Hood is sunshine and storms, forests and fauna; it is snow, ice, and water; it is history and tragedy, mystery and glory.

These pages tell the story of Hood through all of these singular though interconnected facets, each of which could be a tale unto itself. But melded together, the unique aspects of Mount Hood paint a picture of an immense and powerful and alluring mountain with a reach far beyond its forested base, high above its soaring summit.

OFF WE GO

MISTY HERE AT 6,000 FEET *on the south side of Mount Hood. Very misty. In fact, come to think of it, this isn't mist anymore at all. It's real rain and the drops are engorging by the minute. Isn't this August, one of the months it's supposed to be safe to venture outside in Oregon?*

The parking lot here at Timberline Lodge is empty for good reason, but here we are, Amy and I, and our trail hound, Oliver, setting out to tread the Timberline Trail in its entirety. The 41-mile loop encircles the mountain, covers close to 10,000 feet of total elevation gain, tops out at 7,300 feet on the north side, crosses countless streams and rivers, offers views of at least five major Cascade peaks, and attracts thousands of hikers each and every year. And it's been around since 1938.

So in more ways than one, this is the hike to do on Mount Hood.

Although most people knock off the Timberline Trail in three days, I've just been laid off from my reporting gig at a Portland newspaper, freed from work obligations for the time being, and Amy and I like to enjoy ourselves on the trail, so we've budgeted just enough Jack Daniels and Johnny Walker for four evening cocktail hours.

❧

BY THEN, AUGUST 2005, *we'd lived in Portland for eight years and had backpacked all over Oregon and Washington. Mount Hood had become an obvious go-to favorite for us because we lived just an hour's drive away. We'd already spent countless days and nights hiking and camping at places like Burnt Lake, McNeil Point, Elk Meadows, Elk Cove, Cooper Spur, Ramona Falls, Zigzag Mountain, and so on. Last-minute escapes to the Muddy Fork of the Sandy River or Lost Lake were always a weekend option (still are).*

Our original plan for this trip had been to head up to Washington's North Cascades, but logistics and unknowns had made it seem more stressful than such an outing should be. We considered other options too: back to the Wallowas in eastern Oregon, the Three Sisters near Bend, the redwoods. Everywhere, it seemed, but fifty miles east of home.

Amy refocused, however—saw the trees for the forest, if you will—and suggested we give the Timberline Trail a go. Perfect.

EXCEPT FOR THIS RAIN, *which has soaked us damn near through before we even step off the pavement. Even Oliver, who's usually delighted and indifferent to the elements, seems dejected already, droplets beading off his Labrador blackness and drenching his overloaded pack. (I think Amy's stashed her hooch inside it.) But what are you going to do? When else will you have five days off— and then some—to devote to one of the most classic backpacking trails around? This is what we are here to do, the Timberline Trail. And goddamn, we are going to do it.*

The mountain is hidden. The day is soggy, blowing. The massive, seventy-year-old lodge looks quaint and so inviting. I'm sure fires are burning warm and bright within its giant stone fireplaces and hot soup is heating the innards of guests looking out at us through big, bowing windows and thinking, What in the hell are those people doing out there?

Off we go.

DRAWING A MOUNTAIN

*There stood Mount Hood in all the glory of the alpenglow,
looming immensely high, beaming with intelligence, and so
impressive that one was overawed as if suddenly brought
before some superior being newly arrived from the sky.*

—JOHN MUIR, *Steep Trails*

THE FIRST TIME I EVER CLIMBED Mount St. Helens, which
sits about sixty miles northwest of Mount Hood in the
beautiful state of Washington, I found myself picking my way
down the black and tumbled boulders of Monitor Ridge with
a solo vagabond from the East Coast named Mike. Fresh out
of school, bearded and bookish behind thick-framed glasses, he
was on an aimless cross-country exploration. Just himself, his car,
maybe a map, and an open mind. The same kind of journey had
ultimately led Amy and me to Portland back in 1997.

I don't remember many of the words we traded, but one
thing Mike said as the conversation shifted to Mount Hood off
in the distance stuck with me.

If you ask a little kid to draw a mountain, he said, he will draw Mount Hood.

It's such a simplistic way to think about the mountain, but it's true. When he said that, I immediately visualized myself as a second grader—in the flatlands of Ohio, no less—with a fat black pencil scrawling a near-perfect triangle on a piece of paper, then adding a serrated line across its middle to signify the snowcap's end and the beginning of gray bands of rock and green forest below.

THAT'S MOUNT HOOD, from the west anyway, a view that the city of Portland actually helped preserve in its downtown via a handful of building-restricted vista corridors in the 1970s and again in 1991. Looking at it from the north, Hood is steep and sinister, like a shark's tooth, but still beautiful. From the east, it's an elongated dorsal fin of a ridge, a non sequitur to the mountain's symmetrical point on the flip side. And the southern vantage point reveals a stubby bulk littered with the jagged gaps and sharp protrusions that only a volcano can create.

As are its major relations in the Cascade Mountains, which comprise some seventeen prominent summits along a 1,000-mile spine from Lassen Peak in California to just north of Mount Garibaldi in British Columbia, Mount Hood is a *stratovolcano*. Simply put, that means a volcano composed of alternate layers of lava and ash.

Named in 1792 after British admiral Samuel Hood, who never saw the peak but fought against its home country during the Revolutionary War, the roughly 700,000-year-old Hood is somewhat older than many of the other peaks in the range. Its most recent significant eruptive period ran from about 1781 to 1810 and left in its wake Crater Rock, a jaggy lava dome that sits like a scorched thumb at 10,000 feet on the mountain's south face. Locals reported small eruptions of pumice and ash later, in the 1860s, and minor puffs of questionable origin have been reported ever since. The volcano is currently considered dormant, but far from extinct; geologists prefer to say not if, but when. Climbing past Crater Rock today you regularly see steam drifting out of volcanic vents called *fumaroles* and catch sulfury whiffs that add a delightful, dyspeptic tinge to the remaining 1,200-foot climb to the summit.

I know this because I've climbed Mount Hood several times. So have thousands upon thousands of other people. Some 10,000 attempt to climb it each year, making it the second most-climbed mountain in the world. In first comes Japan's 12,388-foot Mount Fuji, which sees an estimated 200,000 prospective sum-miteers every year. New Hampshire's Grand Mount Monadnock, with 125,000 climbers annually, likes to claim that it's actually second in the world to Mount Fuji. And technically it is, but it's kind of hard to drop Mount Hood and Monadnock into the same league, at least with a straight face: Monadnock's summit tops out at just over 3,100 feet.

The most popular route up Hood is the South Side, which starts from Timberline Lodge and trudges—or if you're into the cushy approach, chugs via a snowcat—up the east side of the Palmer Snowfield. From there, it's on up the Palmer (snow-cats dump their loads at about 8,500 feet), around the east side of Crater Rock, up an icy ridge known as the Hogsback, over or around a crevasse called the *bergschrund*, and finally, up an icy chute to the summit. The whole shebang's just three and a half miles—but 5,200 feet of elevation gain—one way.

Most climbs via the South Side route start sometime after midnight so that, if you make the summit, you hit it right around sunrise—absolutely amazing—before the snowcap begins to melt for the day, pelting anyone who's still up there with volleys of rock and ice.

Up there means 11,239 feet above sea level, which makes Mount Hood easily the tallest point in all of Oregon. It's followed by Mount Jefferson to the south, at 10,497 feet, and the 10,358-foot South Sister in Central Oregon west of Bend. It is fourth in line when it comes to Cascadian height, with the 14,411-foot Mount Rainier wearing the crown.

LIKE RAINIER, HOOD is called simply *the mountain* by most who live in its shadow, as in, *I'm going to the mountain today, Did you see the mountain yesterday?* or, during especially prolonged, socked-in gray winters and springs, *Where in the hell is the mountain?* Hood, though, is much smaller than Rainier—the latter holds more glacial ice and snow than all the other Cascades combined—and it's more than 3,000 feet shorter. Rainier's round-the-mountain trail, the Wonderland Trail, is fifty miles longer than Hood's. And climbers looking to get a taste of real cold and real suffering and real weather so that maybe they'll have a chance on Denali or in the Himalayas head not to Mount Hood in the winter—which can nonetheless be brutal in its own right—but to the hulking mass of volcanic enormity that is Mount Rainier.

But if you ask a little kid to draw a mountain, he won't conjure up Rainier's globular greatness. He'll draw a textbook Mount Hood.

Every time.

BEGINNINGS

Youth, what man's age is like to be doth show;
We may our ends by our beginnings know.

—SIR JOHN DENHAM, "Of Prudence"

T HE EARLIEST PAGES of Mount Hood's story begin incomprehensibly long ago—between 500,000 and 700,000 years ago, during the Pleistocene era, which itself began nearly two million years ago. Even earlier, however, geologic forces were at work molding the Northwest landscape.

The High Cascades, a range of high, glaciated mountain peaks whose earliest terrain dates to less than three million years ago, includes Mount Hood and stretches from Lassen Peak in California to north of Mount Garibaldi in British Columbia. The range, which takes its name from long-gone rapids in the Columbia River near Cascade Locks, is actually paralleled in places by an older volcanic spine due west known as the Western Cascades. Tremendous volcanic activity began forming these latter mountains thirty-six million years ago, back when the Willamette Valley was still a sprawling bay of the Pacific Ocean and sharks plied the waters near Eugene. Significant erosion kept these peaks in check, and shifting of the landmass, which drove the ocean ever westward, tilted them on an angle.

Now significantly eroded and forested, the Western Cascades serve as the foothills for the higher summits and are what truly cause the notorious rain shadow of the Cascades. Saturated marine air from the Pacific rises up off these ramping ridgelines until it condenses into wooly gray clouds full of moisture. The result: Oregon's signature rains and quilted skies on the west side of the range, days and days of bluebird sunshine to the east.

Five million years ago, when small camels, elephants, and mastodons still called Oregon home, the Western Cascades rotated even farther westward. This massive movement preceded the birth of a significant new ridgeline of volcanic outpourings, overlapping shield volcanoes and stratovolcanoes, and majestic, peaked formations twenty miles to the east: the High Cascades.

ᕦ

DESPITE ALL ITS FIRE and fractures and floods, geology is much less imaginative than mythology. There's no personification, no jealousy, no sadness. But Native Americans near the Columbia River long ago wove together colorful, adventurous tales to explain the formation of the majestic mountains all around them, never once mentioning volcanic vents or shifting landmasses.

According to the lore of the Klickitat, who lived along the north shores of the Columbia River, native peoples used to be able to cross the river over the sacred Bridge of the Gods. (Various landslides throughout time—one as recent as a few hundred years ago—have actually dammed the river and allowed fleeting passage by foot, so this part of the story may not be entirely legend.) Upset by tribes that began to feud, the Great Spirit first doused all sources of fire, save for the one kept burning by an old and ugly woman named Loowit. She would share her flame with those who came in need of a spark. Pleased by Loowit's kindness, the Great Spirit granted her wish of everlasting youth and beauty. The new dish, however, soon became quite the target, and two of the Great Spirit's sons, Pahto, who ruled the north, and Wy'east in the south, unleashed a terrible war to gain her affection. They hurled fiery boulders at each other and torched the land all around.

Furious at his offspring, the Great Spirit destroyed the bridge over the river and turned all three of the feuding lovers into volcanic peaks: Loowit became the mountain we know today as Mount St. Helens, Pahto is Mount Adams, and Wy'east is Oregon's Mount Hood.

Native American spirits on Hood have also been linked to another geologic manifestation in Oregon: the thunderegg. Oregon's state rock since 1965, the thunderegg is a geologic structure that looks like a plain old rock on the outside; inside, swirling opal and quartz crystals create colorful patterns like galactic nebulae. According to the lore of the Warm Springs tribes on the eastern edge of the Cascades, Thunder Spirits lived high atop Hood and would often clash with their counterparts on Mount Jefferson to the south. During their thunder and lightning battles, the spirits would bean each other with thundereggs stolen from the mythical thunderbird.

❧

EVEN WITHOUT THE warring spirits and jealous lovers, the rise of the High Cascades still boasts some near-mythical proportions. Before Hood and its fiery brethren took their more modern-day shape, ice became king. A worldwide period of chilling and warming two million years ago paved the way for colossal continental ice sheets that spread across North America, Europe, and Asia. A mass of ice nearly a half-mile thick encased the Cascade Range in Oregon from what would become Mount Hood down beyond Mount McLoughlin in southern Oregon. If the massive glaciers that advanced down from Hood during the coldest of these chapters still existed today, the Beer Stube at Mt. Hood Skibowl, Charlie's Mountain View Restaurant & Bar in Government Camp—a small community on the mountain's southern base named for a command of the 1st US Mounted Rifles who abandoned wagons and other supplies there in 1849—and just about everything else down to about 2,500 feet would be entombed in ice.

In between episodes of massive glaciation, volcanic vents along the spine of the High Cascades repeatedly spewed lava and rock fragments that not only created the most prominent Cascade mountains, but also triggered massive floods and mudflows. Near Mount Hood lava flows filled deep, ice-formed canyons and created features like Barrett Spur, an arching ridge on the mountain's northwest flank named after P. G. Barrett, a doctor and early settler of the Hood River Valley. A somewhat smaller volcano, the Sandy Glacier volcano, mostly buried now under Hood's west face but still partially visible above the Muddy Fork of the Sandy River, erupted and oozed lava about 1.3 million years ago.

And then, about 700,000 years ago, the Hood we know today began to erupt in earnest, building itself into a giant andesite and dacite edifice that eventually topped 12,000 feet. Some 100,000 years ago, Hood's entire north side collapsed, unleashing an enormous avalanche that buried the Hood River Valley to the north under 120 feet of rock and mud, laid a hundred-foot-tall dam across the Columbia River, and plowed its way up into the White Salmon River in Washington. Modern-day Hood River, a renowned windsurfing and kiteboarding mecca north of Hood and home to nearly 7,000 people, is built atop these volcanic remnants.

A massive ice cap again encased Hood about 25,000 years ago, but the mountain continued to grow. Lava domes, including the Steel Cliff on Hood's southeast face, thrust up around the summit. The upper 2,000 feet of the mountain likely emerged while Hood was still smothered during this last Ice Age, though the ice eventually winnowed the mountain's summit down by almost 1,000 feet. And then, about 15,000 years ago, the sprawling ice sheets that had mantled the mountain for millennia began their long, slow retreat back up the hill.

SUCCESSIVE ERUPTIONS of Hood were dominated not by powerful explosions, but by the rise and collapse of small lava domes. Unlike Mount St. Helens to the north, which has repeatedly and violently blown its top over the past 50,000 years, and other surrounding Cascades like Jefferson and the Three Sisters, Hood does not appear to have had an exceptionally explosive history. Scientists like Willie Scott, a geologist at the David A. Johnston Cascades Volcano Observatory (CVO) in Vancouver, Washington, know this not because of what they've found around the mountain but, rather, because of what's missing.

"Around St. Helens, there are thick deposits of coarse ash and pumice," said Scott, who's spent nearly thirty years at the CVO with Hood as one of his main areas of research. "We find precious little of that at Hood. Ash from St. Helens has been found in Canada, but at Hood we just don't get that."

Instead, Mount Hood ash tends to be very fine and usually sticks close to the mountain, piling up in thick blankets near its base, particularly over on the east side. Around Hood there's also very little pumice, the porous and often buoyant volcanic rock that accompanies most sustained explosive eruptions. All of this suggests that Hood's volcanic activity has been marked more by the building and collapse of volcanic domes, *pyroclastic flows* 60 mph avalanches of superheated rock and gas—and volcanic mudflows known as *lahars*, than by the turbulent explosions associated with other Cascade peaks.

"There's a reason for that but we just don't know it yet," said Scott, suggesting that during past eruptions, gas in Hood's lava has for one reason or another deflated by the time it's made its way to the surface. "Hood is just the gentle giant."

IN ITS MORE RECENT geological past of the prior 2,000 years, Hood sustained three eruptive periods. The Timberline period, about 1,800 years ago, saw a tremendous collapse of Hood's then steep southern side and the exposure of a main volcanic vent. From this vent and its surrounds, dome-building and collapse ensued on into the Zigzag period about 600 years ago. This construction and destruction unleashed repeated pyroclastic flows and lahars that left in their wake the smooth fan of debris that now dominates the southern face. Timberline Lodge and the community of Government Camp sit atop this erupted detritus. The most recent period, known as the Old Maid, rumbled from the 1760s to about 1810 and created one of the youngest and most prominent features on Hood's southern mug, the 550-foot-tall dacite dome known as Crater Rock that has plugged up the volcano's most recently active major vent.

"You probably could have sat through that eruption at Timberline Lodge and been OK," said Scott.

Since then, however, the mountain has kept relatively quiet even though there have been various reports of unrest over the years. Newspaper accounts in the *Oregonian* told of "an occasional flash of fire" and the seeming disappearance of part of the northwest side of the mountain on August 20, 1859; the September 26, 1865, edition carried a report that the summit of Hood had been "enveloped in smoke and flame. Yes sir, real jets of flame . . . accompanied by discharge of what appeared to be fragments of rock."

Scott doesn't discount such reports outright, but a lack of corresponding volcanic deposits keeps him and his longtime colleague Cynthia Gardner, scientist-in-charge at the CVO, fairly skeptical of those and other specious accounts.

"In any given year, we get reports of eruptions in the Cascades," Gardner said. "People are tremendously passionate about it. It could be alpenglow or weather-related or steam. The best we can do is think that maybe something happened back then, but there are just no appreciable deposits for real proof."

۶€

GARDNER AND SCOTT may know Mount Hood, geologically anyway, better than anyone else around. Both had been part of a five-person team of USGS scientists studying volcano hazards in the early 1980s from an office in, of all places, Denver. After the eruption of Mount St. Helens in 1980, federal funding for volcano monitoring and research jumped tenfold and the USGS permanently established the CVO in Vancouver, Washington. A year after the observatory's founding, the USGS named it in honor of David Johnston, the USGS volcanologist who'd radioed, "Vancouver! Vancouver! This is it!" from Coldwater Ridge seconds before the lateral blast from St. Helens on May 18, 1980, killed him and fifty-six others.

Scott, Gardner, and the rest of the volcano hazards group all transferred up to the Vancouver observatory between 1985 and 1987. At the time, the Survey, as it's called by those who work for it, had long been studying and mapping the Cascades for potential geothermal resources. That effort meshed well with the goals of the volcano scientists, who were interested in learning more about the structure and eruptive history of the volcanoes. Having already mapped a fifteen-mile chain of volcanoes south of Mount Bachelor with Gardner, Scott wanted to take on a bigger mapping project. Hood fit the bill.

Starting in 1989, he and Gardner began traipsing all around the mountain, poring over old lava flows and lahars and mapping surface elements based on age and type of material. They explored remote and beautiful places, some of which were much more accessible back then via roads that have since been decommissioned under new wilderness designations. In their wanderings, they came upon pristine waterfalls on the east side of the volcano and bushwhacked through the thickest parts of the surrounding forest to size up the mountain's base.

Their effort was doubly difficult because in 1989, all the two geologists had to go on were compasses, altimeters, and topographic maps that didn't depict much detail below the canopy of trees; they had no GPS, and definitely no maps made with Light Detection and Ranging (LIDAR) technology, which uses lasers to produce detailed elevation models of the earth's surface sans annoying little hindrances like giant Douglas fir trees. Unfortunately for Scott and Gardner, much of Hood's lower portions are well below timberline, meaning that they spent a fair amount of time wandering in the woods trying to figure out exactly where they were.

"When you look at the outline of Mount Hood, there's this glorious part that everybody recognizes above tree line," Scott said. "Well, that's a pretty small percentage of the volcano. Most of it is down in the trees, in a deep, dark, rhododendron-infested jungle."

What you see from Portland, Scott added, when you're distracted by the beautiful white peak gleaming off in the distance in the early summer sunshine, are volcanic rocks that are roughly 300,000 years old; down below the tree line, they range from 500,000 to 600,000 years or older. The entire mass is something in the neighborhood of ten to twelve miles in diameter.

Scott and Gardner's resultant map, still a work in progress thanks to various duties that have pulled the geologists away from the task over the years—like tending to the reawakening of St. Helens in 2004—looks like a psychedelic lily, swirled with different colors, each one representing a specific eruptive history on

Mount Hood. Scott likens the map, which depicts Hood as if you were above it and looking down, to a pie with an opening in the center that's spewed successive layers of eruptive filling over the past 700 centuries or so.

VOLCANO

I once had a guy from New York come up to me and say,
"All this stuff about Mount Hood being a volcano—you
buy that?"

—Jon Tullis, Timberline Lodge

B EYOND THE SIMPLE FACT that the gigantic mass of mountain off on the horizon is a volcano, signs of Mount Hood's eruptive history and potential are everywhere. Climb the monster up its southern slopes and you start smelling the rotten eggs of hydrogen sulfide halfway up. A little higher, near Crater Rock, at the Devil's Kitchen and the Hot Rocks area around 10,000 feet, steam and sulfur stench drift in thin tendrils out of fumaroles. The ground temperature around these vents has been recorded at about 185 degrees Fahrenheit; the fumaroles themselves run up to 198 degrees Fahrenheit, about fourteen degrees shy of what it takes to boil a pot of water.

But one need not climb high up on Hood to sense the forces that bore the mountain. Occasionally you can catch a whiff of eau de sulfur in the Timberline Lodge parking lot—4,000 feet below the vents of Hood's upper reaches. Camp along the banks of the Muddy Fork of the Sandy River at Old Maid Flat, an area once buried under fifty feet of Timberline- and Old Maid–era sediment, and many of the boulders you scramble over, the rocks you use for a fire ring or toss into the silty current, were likely high up on or deep inside of Mount Hood just a few hundred years ago. A triangular lump of this rock, dark gray lava swirled with maroon and speckled white, sits on the windowsill above my desk, a gift from my four-year-old daughter after one of many sunny afternoons spent on the river at Old Maid Flat.

The most recent significant eruption, pegged at late 1781 or early 1782, escaped from the vent near Crater Rock and sent a lahar down the Sandy, bowling over and burying forests of towering cedars and firs, all the way to the river's confluence with the Columbia River fifty-six miles away. Many of these snags are plainly visible today along the trail to Ramona Falls and rising up like tombstones out of nearby Lost Creek. So inundated with mud and debris was the river from this same lahar that, thirteen years later, when Lewis and Clark came upon its mouth at the Columbia River, they christened it the Quicksand River, a name later shortened to the Sandy.

Bone-white stumps and trunks of whitebark pines, killed instantly by an eruptive surge of hot gas and ash from the circa 1780 episode, lay scattered like bones across a ridge above timberline just west of Mt. Hood Meadows Ski Resort. Down below, in the bottom of White River Canyon, sit snags overrun by the eruption—one of six such buried forests around the mountain that bear witness to the past 2,000 years of the peak's volcanic activity. In addition to those on the upper Sandy River and in White River Canyon, buried forests have been found and can be seen above Paradise Park at 5,800 feet—the Stadter buried forest, smothered by lahars and pyroclastic flows about 1,700 years ago— along the Zigzag River near the old Twin Bridges Campground and the Tollgate Wayside, and fifty miles away along the banks of the Sandy River outside of Troutdale near Oxbow Regional Park.

Farther from the mountain toward Portland, direct fallout from Hood's past eruptions is less evident. But there is plenty around to keep the volcanism that built the mountain and the entire region close to people's everyday thoughts. Portland landmarks like Powell Butte and Rocky Butte—a city dweller's quick fix for climbing—rose from vents in the Boring volcanic field less than a million years ago, when Hood was itself beginning to burble. Shooting a three-pointer on the court at Mount Tabor Park, a characteristic Portland gem, puts you squarely on top of the vent that built the 643-foot cinder cone of the same name. And if ever in early August you head to the Pendarvis Farm in Happy Valley, just outside southeast Portland, for the fantastic three-day music festival known as Pickathon, you'll be swaying to the tunes on the eastern flanks of Mount Scott, an extinct volcano named for Harvey Scott, editor of the *Oregonian,* in 1889.

Even though all that happened long, long ago, and even though the mountain has piped down over the past two centuries—something akin to an hour ago in geologic terms— Hood is still considered one of the most dangerous volcanoes in the United States. It ranks number four on a USGS top ten list based on size and potential damage of an eruption. Ahead of Hood in order of danger: Mount Rainier, which looms over the entire Puget Sound region and its more than four million residents; St. Helens, the most active Cascade volcano in modern history; and, at number one, Kilauea, which has been erupting continuously on the Big Island of Hawaii since 1983.

When Hood decides to party again, it will probably show up much as it's done in the recent past: not explosively, but with a collapse or outburst near Crater Rock that will send pyroclastic flows and lahars down the mountain's southern flanks.

"For volcanic hazards, the past is key to the future," Gardner said. "It's not a one-to-one correlation, but it's pretty critical to understand that past eruptive history to get a sense of what could happen when the volcano reawakens."

Though the likely scenario for the next eruption parallels what happened 200 years ago, the stakes have changed just a bit since then. Unlike during the 1780s, when Hood had yet to even be seen by the white man, there are now five ski areas around the mountain, one irreplaceable historic lodge at 6,000 feet visited by nearly two million people a year, a handful of communities and several thousand people in the direct line of pyroclastic fire and lahars, key highway corridors surrounding the mountain, and more than 2.2 million people living within the major metropolitan area around Portland, a figure that's expected to grow by more than a million people by 2030. In addition, more than 500 cargo and commercial flights—many of which soar right past Hood and cause untold numbers of jaws to drop—take off or land at Portland International Airport every day. And hundreds of ships make their way every year up the Columbia River, a major water transport route that closed for a week when sediments from the Mount St. Helens eruption of May 18, 1980, clogged its main channel.

In short, an eruption on Mount Hood could be big.

In the most likely scenario, according to an emergency response document known as *The Mount Hood Coordination Plan*, an eruption and/or collapse at Crater Rock would unleash pyroclastic flows that could steamroll nearly six miles down the south side of the mountain in about ten minutes, burning and burying everything along the way. Bye-bye Magic Mile ski lift, Silcox Hut, Timberline Lodge, and possibly even the outskirts of Government Camp. They could also light up the forest trees like matchsticks. Complementary lava flows, while not an immediate threat ("They tend to move down the valley at a slow enough pace that they're almost a tourist attraction," Gardner said), could also set the surrounding forest ablaze. The initial eruption would also fire ballistic fragments like cannonballs for up to three miles, far enough to pummel cars or people in the parking lot at Timberline.

As happened on Mount St. Helens, which lost seventy percent of its glacial ice mass to the May 18, 1980, eruption, torrential snow and ice melt floods could barrel down the mountain, and lahars, some up to one hundred feet deep, could choke the Sandy, Zigzag, White, and Salmon River valleys. The mudflows are what pose the greatest threat to nearby communities. In about three hours, a lahar might flow fifty-six miles down the Sandy River to the Columbia River, plowing over key roads—there's a good chance that Highway 26, the main route over Hood's south side pass, would have to be closed—bridges, and the last few remaining above-ground sections of conduit that feed Portland its drinking water from the Bull Run watershed. The increased sediment in the Columbia would probably stymie shipping and give homeowners along the north shore of the river good reason to leave: more sediment in the river means more erosion and, subsequently, less shorefront to anchor riverfront homes. And parts of Highway 35 on the east side of Mount Hood, which has taken its fair share of beatings from mountain floods and debris flows even without any kind of eruptive activity, could be barreled over and yet again washed down the valley like so much sand out to sea.

According to another USGS document, *Volcano Hazards in the Mount Hood Region*, the best way to steer clear of these lahars in the case of an eruption is to get to higher ground right quick. But if you hear a loud roaring noise, "like a gradually approaching jet plane," you might want to get your affairs in order: that would be a lahar just around the corner.

Though there probably wouldn't be a towering ash column from Hood's next eruption, pyroclastic flows and surges can produce their own ash clouds that rise thousands of feet in the air. Ash from such clouds, known as *tephra*, would darken the sky, rain down on fleeing drivers, smother vegetation, damage airliners' jet engines, and likely sideline air traffic in and out of Portland International Airport. The eruption of Iceland's Eyjafjallajökull in the late spring of 2010 did just that, disrupting flights across Europe for weeks. Tephra clouds also short-circuit power lines and cause lightning strikes that wreak havoc on communication systems. The same ash would probably find its way into the Bull Run watershed, something that happened during St. Helens's outburst in 1980, and temporarily render the water too turbid for Portlanders to drink.

All of this makes for an almost overwhelming lot to think about should Hood rumble back to life. But on top of all the hot gases, ash, mudflows, floods, and other fire and brimstone that Hood has in store for northwest Oregon, there's something else to consider: how long an eruption might last. Although the cataclysmic eruption of St. Helens on May 18, 1980, gets all the press, that was simply the climax of several months of unrest—and the prelude to nearly six more years of continual volcanic dyspepsia. Mount Hood's own Old Maid eruptive period lasted for a couple decades. On the Big Island of Hawaii, Kilauea has been oozing lava almost continuously since 1983, and the ongoing eruption of the Soufrière Hills volcano on the Caribbean island of Montserrat, which has killed at least nineteen people, buried the capital city of Plymouth in up to forty feet of ash, and forced 7,000 of the island's 11,000 inhabitants to flee altogether, began in 1995 and had yet to completely settle down as of 2010.

"There is the persistence factor to consider, where the effects are not just a disruption," Gardner said of a possible eruption of Hood. "A long, persistent eruption would wipe out a community—and it's not going to come back."

BECAUSE VOLCANIC ERUPTIONS are low-frequency, high-consequence events, emergency managers throughout the region have the difficult job of planning a response for something they may never see in their lifetimes. *The Mount Hood Coordination Plan* outlines a reawakening scenario and a general response plan for emergency managers leading up to, throughout, and after an eruption. While there won't be any whaling emergency sirens like the seventeen in place in communities that lie in the direct path of potential lahars around Mount Rainier, should Mount Hood begin to stir, the USGS would immediately issue updates and alerts similar to those of the National Weather Service or

Homeland Security, from the benign "normal" all the way up to a head-for-the-hills "warning."

Scientists would do this from a temporary volcanic observatory headquartered in Sandy. The entire response would be guided by a unified command of officials from the USGS, the Forest Service, FEMA, local counties, and the Confederated Tribes of Warm Springs.

The thirty-one page document also lays out in general terms what each jurisdiction's role would be in case of an eruption, from monitoring the volcano to sharing information with concerned residents and evacuating them if a blast seems imminent.

This latter task may be among the most difficult, as people don't particularly care to be removed from their homes for an extended period of time. Just before St. Helens went ape in 1980, residents were evacuated, but not without some resistance. On May 17, the day before the eruption, authorities granted evacuated residents a window to head back to their homes to retrieve their belongings. To placate residents further, another opportunity was scheduled for the morning of Sunday, May 18, but the mountain put the kibosh on that one when it blew at 8:32 a.m. In the buildup to the eruption, Harry Truman, the infamous bourbon-drinking owner of the Mt. St. Helens Lodge on Spirit Lake, simply refused to leave his home no matter what, even though catastrophe was all but certain. He and his sixteen cats are now thought to be buried in ash and debris 150 feet under the modern-day Spirit Lake just north of the St. Helens crater.

❧

FORTUNATELY FOR THOSE who live in the shadow of potentially active volcanoes like some of the Cascades, modern monitoring methods keep a pretty good watch over what's going on. In a back room at the CVO, various seismic readings come in constantly from Pacific Northwest Seismic Network instruments that measure and record seismic movement, including earthquakes, on Cascade volcanoes such as Mount Hood, Adams, Baker, Crater Lake, Glacier Peak, Rainier, St. Helens, and the Three Sisters. Though most of the information is digital now and even available online almost daily, jaggy little pens still record some data on drums of paper known as *helicorders*. To a layman such as myself looking at all the sharp peaks and valleys running across digital screens and spools of white paper, it looked like every major Cascade was about to blow, but Scott assured me all was normal. Scientists who know what to look for in a seismograph reading can usually tell the difference between, say, a snowcat starting its engine near a monitoring station by Timberline Lodge and an earthquake that could send Hood erupting anew.

Pinned on the wall like a dorm room poster was a huge printout from the September 23, 2004, reawakening of Mount St. Helens. In the days leading up to the unrest, the lines were relatively straight and steady with just an occasional jump here and there. Then came September 23, when the instruments detected a swarm of 200 very minor earthquakes in a fifteen-hour span, the kind of mass movement that often serves as prelude to an eruption. More serrated outbursts began to spark across the page, increasing daily until the readouts looked like rows of colored stalagmites. They all blurred together in a frenetic outburst on

October 1, when St. Helens blasted a steam explosion 12,000 feet into the atmosphere and again on October 5, when it sent a column of volcanic ash to similar heights.

Scientists also monitor volcanic gases on the mountains and use satellites and delicate ground instruments to detect any land deformations or swelling that could portend an eruption. In 2001 new satellite imagery revealed that a land area just south of South Sister, a 10,358-foot Cascade volcano in central Oregon, had slowly risen about four inches. Because the area measured close to ten miles in diameter, its rise went unnoticed on the ground. But once the satellite image confirmed the uplift—likely caused by magma moving deep underground—a minor frenzy ensued. People called and wanted to see it. The media posited all kinds of eruption scenarios and, much to the chagrin and humor of the CVO scientists, took to calling the nearly imperceptible uplift a "bulge." Gardner recalled one conversation between a snappy CVO receptionist and a male reporter looking to talk to a scientist:

> Reporter: *Hi, we're calling because we want to talk about the bulge.*
>
> Receptionist: *It's four inches. I wouldn't call that a bulge.*
>
> Reporter, after awkward silence: *Just like a woman.*

By 2004 the uplift in question had simmered down and the media had moved on.

ALTHOUGH MOUNT HOOD has remained relatively quiet in recent times, it does shudder a fair amount itself. Seismic monitors have been recording regular small earthquakes on and around the mountain for more than thirty years; the tally as of 2006 was about 1,400 quakes within five miles of the mountain. On a Friday morning in May 2010, a swarm of quakes, one of which clocked in at a magnitude of 3.0, rattled the peak. In 2003 a magnitude 3.3 quake struck, and in 2002 the mountain experienced more than 200 earthquakes over a three-month period, most of them about four miles underneath Mt. Hood Meadows Ski Resort. One of those, a 4.5-magnitude temblor that marked the strongest one since a 4.0 in the early 1970s, shuddered through workers at Timberline Lodge.

Though scientists don't know exactly what causes these tremors, they believe it has something to do either with a series of underground faults or subtle changes in the subterranean magma chambers far below the mountain. Either way, one earthquake or a swarm of many earthquakes do not an eruption make. They are actually par for the course on most volcanoes.

However, earthquakes can often be one of the first indications of an aberration on the way. Two months before the 1980 blast that chopped 1,300 feet off the height of Mount St. Helens, a magnitude 4.2 earthquake grumbled underneath its slopes. Two months later, after the north side of the mountain had begun to bulge, a flurry of earthquakes, capped by one with a magnitude of 5.1, rocked the mountain. The quakes touched off the largest known debris avalanche in recorded history, a lateral blast and pyroclastic flow that bowled over 230 square miles of timber like so many toothpicks, and a nearly twenty-mile column of ash that towered into the middle of the stratosphere.

That, in part, is why scientists who monitor volcanoes play such close attention to earthquakes. Along with keeping an eye on the gases that volcanoes emit and any changes in the terrain on or around a volcano, tracking a mountain's earthquakes gives scientists a pretty good hand when it comes to detecting—not predicting—unrest. When St. Helens began to shimmy again on September 23, 2004, with more than 200 small quakes in just fifteen hours, and then kept it up for several more days, the scientists knew something was up. But until that point, nothing seemed amiss.

And that's the rub for scientists like Scott, Gardner, and their CVO colleagues whose charge is to keep their fingers on the pulse of a potentially destructive peak like Mount Hood and let the rest of us know—preferably to the exact date and very well in advance so we can plan accordingly—when it's going to blow its mind. The nice thing about Mount Hood is that, because it's been essentially dormant for roughly 200 years, the conduit system that would feed magma toward the surface has likely solidified. That system would have to fracture and reopen before any major engines could start to rev again, and that's the kind of activity that geologists are probably not going to miss. Still, trying to predict when that next eruption could happen—and how severe it could be—is like looking into a crystal ball.

"You could make a great contribution to society if you could figure that out," Scott said.

Even so, at the end of an hours-long discussion about the mountain with the two veteran geologists, who seemed to know and relish the volcanology of the Cascades like a colorful family history, I simply had to throw out the quintessential, make-the-scientists'-eyes-roll question about Mount Hood: Is it going to erupt again anytime soon?

They both chuckled, like they'd heard it before and knew it was coming.

"The odds are, we're not going to see it," Gardner said, immediately qualifying her answer. "But tomorrow, it could start. Somebody could have asked the night before September 23, 2004, 'What are the odds of St. Helens starting up again tomorrow?' and most of us would not have put money down on it. That's the reality for us: that until the volcano chooses to give us some indication that unrest is beginning, things motor on and are just fine. And then one day they aren't fine anymore."

RAIN AND A RIVER

JUST A FEW MILES IN *and we're soaked through. It's not really even rain now, just unrelenting mist and steady breezes that keep it blowing from all sides, saturating the surface of everything like a paint sprayer. It's easy to start dreading five days of this: Did I bring warm enough clothes? How about the tarp so we're not holed up in the tent every single night? Amy looks kind of dry in her rain pants. Maybe I should have brought more Gore-Tex and less Hemingway. Can't wait for that burger and beer at Calamity Jane's.*

Drip.

We don't talk much, and what with the clouds socking everything in, there's little to see save for the droplets drip, drip, dripping off the corn lilies and bear grass and strands of old-man's beard lichen draped on the branches overhead. At least Oliver's having fun. Now that he's on the trail and able to bound, his step has sprung and he's not bothered at all by the water that's beading off his coat as he races up and back, up and back.

As we're climbing back up out of Zigzag Canyon, the sky starts to dry up, and so do we. A little sunshine even, and the clouds that have been blanketing the alpine terrain above begin to break up. Amazing what a little change in the weather can do for the soul. We start shedding miles along with our rain gear, and by the time we're at mile ten and crossing the Sandy River, the sky has lightened up to near-blue. A perfect spot to stop for the night, overlooking the Sandy, nobody else around, even the historic Upper Sandy Guard Station just up the hill for exploring.

After we set up for the evening, I check out the old stone and log cabin that the city of Portland and the Forest Service built in 1935 as part of Roosevelt's New Deal. Its main purpose at the time was to keep hikers on the Timberline Trail from straying into the Bull Run watershed, the source of Portland's drinking water. It's charming, but also dilapidated from seventy years of mountain life. A sign on the wall warning of potential bubonic plague or some other medieval-sounding disease sends me back down to camp for cocktail hour. We unwind over dinner, catch the rise of a blazing white moon somewhere up toward the mountain, and zip in for an early day tomorrow that will take us back to one of the most amazing waterfalls on the entire mountain for the first time in seven years.

WATER

Then shall the lame man leap as a hart, and the tongue
of the dumb sing: for in the wilderness shall waters
break out, and streams in the desert. And the parched
ground shall become a pool, and the thirsty land springs
of water . . .

—ISAIAH 35:6–7

Our very first backpacking trip on Mount Hood
found four of us—Amy, me, and two friends, Mark and
Christina—making our way along the Sandy River during the
muggy summer solstice of 1998. These were the early, formative
days of our wilderness camping, so our packs were stuffed like
turkeys. In with my normal gear, I had a big kerosene lantern, a
honking hatchet, a couple books, a notebook, and more wine than
remotely necessary. Mark's girlfriend ended up not being able to
join us, but he lugged food for two anyway: baked potatoes, a
whole stick of butter, a couple beers. He also had a circus tent of
a tarp, a six-inch survival knife—the Rambo kind with the compass in the handle and the camouflage sheath—and an old-school

sleeping bag, all of it packed in or hanging from a giant borrowed and blue pack that looked like a suitcase with shoulder straps. So full and towering were our packs that one passerby asked us if we were hiking the entire Pacific Crest Trail—a 2,600-mile trek that stretches from Mexico to Canada.

Our loads made what would normally have been a tame three-and-a-half-mile trail feel more like ten. The unseasonably thick and humid air didn't help much, nor did the clouds of fine dust billowing up off the trail. But the cool, silvery waters of the Sandy paralleling the route and the occasional glimpses up the glacial valley to Mount Hood helped displace the burden. And just as we got close to where we were going, the weight lifted, and nothing else really mattered.

At first, just distant hissing and dripping up ahead; then louder. Through the still trees, white and misty movement against a dark shadow. We lumbered up the rest of the trail, eased off our packs, and looked up.

Ramona Falls.

QUITE POSSIBLY the most beautiful cascade on all of Mount Hood—I'd even suggest in all the Northwest—Ramona Falls is 120 feet of waterfall splendor, the clear waters of an unseen glacial stream up above cascading down and fanning out across the jumbled black basalt of a long-ago lava flow. Standing before it inspires serenity, peaceful beauty, and appreciation of all that is naturally grand. Tasting its waters is like drinking a snowy mountain wind.

In August 1933, John Mills, a US Forest Service employee who supervised some of the Civilian Conservation Corps trail projects around Mount Hood, came upon the falls while plotting a trail. Lovesick at the time for a woman who would become his wife, Mills found his mind consumed by a popular song of the day called simply *Ramona*. Written by L. Wolfe Gilbert and Mabel Wayne, the song accompanied a 1928 movie of the same name made to depict an 1884 novel by Helen Hunt Jackson about racism in Southern California. From the song's refrain:

Ramona, when day is done you'll hear my call

Ramona, we'll meet beside the waterfall.

I dread the dawn when I awake to find you gone

Ramona, I need you, my own

Though since recorded by everyone from Louis Armstrong to the Everly Brothers, the original recording, by the alluring Mexican film star Delores del Rio in 1928, remains the quintessential version. I found a grainy and scratchy recording of it, and from first listen the song has stuck with me and reminded me constantly of a beautiful waterfall on Mount Hood.

RAMONA FALLS may very well be the most aesthetic expression of water on Mount Hood, though fans of Tamanawas Falls or Eliot Creek or the crystalline waters of the Salmon River may beg to differ. It's also just a tiny fraction of all the water that cascades down, melts off of, seeps out of, rains down on, or otherwise runs off the mountain and its surrounding forested foothills. The point being that not only is there no shortage of liquid beauty that counts Mount Hood as its source or influence, but that the mountain and its surrounds are responsible for an enormous—and essential—volume of water.

Enormous, in that the million-acre Mount Hood National Forest's average annual flow of water, which includes five major drainages, is something in the order of six million acre-feet or nearly two trillion gallons of water per year. Add up all the surface water across the entire forest—bodies like lakes, springs, and creeks, including 5,000 miles of perennial and intermittent streams—and the sum is up near 71,000 acres, an area about half the size of Lake Tahoe. Behind all that water is primarily rain and snow. The mountain itself can get up to 500 inches of snow every year, and annual average precipitation at lower levels can range anywhere from 40 inches to more than 200.

Five prominent rivers link directly to the mountain: the Salmon, Zigzag, Sandy, Hood, and White, all of which start their days as silty glacial runoff high up on Hood and eventually become part of the mighty Columbia River to the north. From its headwaters at the Palmer Snowfield, the thirty-three-mile Salmon winds a long and circuitous way down the mountain, through a soaring forest of old-growth firs and cedars and a series of gushing waterfalls with names like Frustration, Final, and Vanishing that are easier heard than seen. Host to wild cutthroat and winter steelhead and chinook, the Salmon is one of the only rivers in the country to be designated a National Wild and Scenic River for its entire course, though stretches of Hood's four other major rivers enjoy similar designation. To reach the Columbia, both the Salmon and the twelve-mile Zigzag River flow into the Sandy River low in Hood's western foothills near Brightwood—a community named for the way sunlight reflects off its cottonwood trees—and Zigzag, respectively. The Sandy, Hood's longest river at fifty-six miles, actually picks up no fewer than eighteen streams and rivers along its way to the Columbia.

Although the Sandy and Zigzag rivers have at times made life interesting for nearby residents—both rivers flooded after a warm rain storm in January 2011, wiping out sections of road, bowling over trees, and washing away at least three homes—the forty-nine-mile White River on Hood's southeast side is perhaps the mountain's most troublesome, at least to the Oregon Department of Transportation engineers who have to rebuild Highway 35 every time the river washes it out. Native Americans who populated sites along the Columbia River, including the Tenino tribe, are known to have fished, hunted, and gathered plants along the banks of the White River more than 10,000 years ago.

And before the river that forms in three branches from Hood's north- and east-side glaciers became known as the Hood River, it was called Dog River. Short on food, a band of starving pioneers in the area resorted to eating dog meat, and somehow the river took the canine moniker. Finding the name distasteful, Mary Coe, wife of Nathaniel Coe, founder of the city of Hood River, successfully petitioned to have it changed to Hood River in the 1850s. A small tributary of the East Fork Hood River, however, still bears the name Dog River.

In addition to the fish and other wildlife that rely on Hood's water sources, Oregonians use the agua on and around Mount Hood in endless ways. They fish and swim, paddle, camp, and chill on and along its rivers and streams; the same goes for its popular lakes like Lost, Trillium—both of which feature classic vistas of the mountain—Timothy, Clear, Mirror, Badger, and Burnt. The Mt. Hood Brewing Co. in Government Camp boasts that its beers are brewed with the mountain's pure glacial water, though it's likely been filtered and lightly treated since most glacial run-off is, at its source, cloudy with ground-up debris of all make and manner. The water source for Timberline Lodge is a spring more than a mile below the lodge that also feeds the Salmon River's west fork. Orchardists in the drier Hood River Valley use water melting off the mountain to give life to their 15,000 acres of pears, apples, and cherries. In the late nineteenth century, logging companies used the Sandy River as a giant floating conveyor belt to move logs and railroad ties—sometimes by the tens of thousands in a single drive—from their mills near Brightwood to awaiting steam trains in Troutdale.

The churning waters of the Sandy and Little Sandy rivers, the Hood River, and the White River at its impressive White River Falls, have also all been harnessed to generate electricity for nearby communities, though that's dimmed some over the years. The White River Falls power station turned its lights out in 1960 at the completion of The Dalles Dam across the Columbia, and the Sandy River became an entirely free-flowing river for the first time in ninety years in 2007 when Portland General Electric decommissioned its Marmot Dam. At the same time, the power company also broke the hearts of longtime local residents by removing its dam on the Little Sandy River, which drained the popular, hundred-year-old Roslyn Lake in four days.

Oregonians also consume water from all around Mount Hood—more than fifty-four billion gallons of it every year based on Forest Service estimates. According to the USFS, 98 percent of the Mount Hood National Forest is somebody's municipal drinking water supply. The forest is home to at least fifteen municipal watersheds that slake the thirst and water the gardens of people throughout the region, from Hood River and The Dalles to Sandy, Lake Oswego, and the biggest guzzler of all based on sheer size, Portland.

HARD TO BELIEVE that the primary source of drinking water for more than 860,000 Oregonians—more than 20 percent of the entire state—is, at its headwaters in the northwestern foothills of Mount Hood, little more than a shallow, translucent stream just a few feet wide. Named after the runaway cattle that chased land surveyors through the nearby forest in the late 1800s, the Bull Run River emanates from a serene mountain lake of the same name with an immaculate shot of Mount Hood rising over its eastern end. When conditions are right, the lake reflects the face of the mountain like a mirror.

Water seeps out of the lake, disappears briefly into the porous volcanic underground, and then burbles back up about a quarter of a mile later amidst the green moss and ferns, towering Douglas firs, hemlocks, and cedars that thrive deep within the Bull Run watershed. Not many people get to see Bull Run Lake in person—or fantasize what it would be like to call one of the three leftover cabins there home—nor do many get to stroll down to the banks of the Bull Run River near its origins. The entire 102-square-mile watershed, 95 percent of which lies within the Mount Hood National Forest, is off-limits to the public. In fact, all 147 square miles of the Bull Run Watershed Management Unit, which surrounds and includes the watershed, is closed to just about everyone save for select employees of the Portland

Water Bureau, the US Forest Service, Portland General Electric, and any contractors who may be working within its borders.

This all started in the late 1800s, when Portlanders in search of a new source of water for their burgeoning city identified the watershed twenty-six miles to the east as their best option, the Willamette River and Oswego Lake being too polluted, the Clackamas River logistically too far away. President Benjamin Harrison set aside the watershed as the nation's fifth forest preserve in 1892—a precursor to the national forest system—and on January 2, 1895, after an engineering marvel that involved road building, mule and horse trains hauling massive pipes through feet of sucking mud, and a fortuitous dose of gravity that still powers most of the system today, water from the Bull Run River flowed into Portland for the very first time. In 1904, prompted by threats to the watershed from sheep grazing and reckless campers, President Theodore Roosevelt signed the Bull Run Trespass Act, prohibiting public access into the watershed.

But I found a way in.

Unlike the fishermen or skinny dippers who occasionally sneak in to prime spots along the river, my way in was hardly surreptitious. For water nerds, engaged citizens, and a few writers here and there, the Portland Water Bureau offers a limited number of daylong tours of the watershed. In true Portland fashion, these excursions to tour the municipal water system book up fast and early. I called in May and barely got a seat for mid-July.

When I talked to Jody Burlin, a water resources educator with the bureau, about the tour and why I wanted to go, she shared with me some news I already knew: despite the fact that the Bull Run watershed lies within the mountain's namesake national forest and sits in glorious eyesight of the snowy summit, Mount Hood is not the source of Portland's drinking water.

~~❧~~

THERE IS A COMMON misconception among many Portlanders that Mount Hood serves as a giant tap for their drinking water. It's an understandable, if technically erroneous, assumption. They see all that white snow up there, the purifying forests, the crystalline streams that run from its flanks, and think, of course that's what's coming out of my faucet, hydrating my organic arugula and slaking my parched palate after one too many IPAs or pinot noirs.

But technically, Mount Hood proper does not provide the Rose City with a single drop of water for drinking. When then Oregon governor Sylvester Pennoyer proclaimed during the planning of Bull Run that Hood's glacial waters would "cause goiter to the fair sex of Portland," he was not only advocating for a water system run by a private enterprise—one in which he reportedly had a hand in—but he was also proliferating a common misunderstanding that Bull Run Lake and Bull Run River are fed by the glaciers and snow that blanket Mount Hood.

In reality, the watershed feeds mainly on Oregon's notorious rain. If Portland can seem eternally gray and saturated with its thirty-six to forty inches of rainfall every year, imagine living out by Bull Run, where triple the raindrops fall from the sky for an annual average soaking of some 130 inches; at the higher elevations, it can be more like 170 inches. The watershed, which ranges in elevation from 750 feet to 4,700 feet, does get buried under snow every winter, and fog drip adds a tad here and there, but it is the storied Northwest rains that provide 90 to 95 percent of the Bull Run's water.

Furthermore, a sizeable ridge stands between Mount Hood and Bull Run, keeping the mountain's glacial runoff from mingling with the Bull Run's water. Not until the glacially fed Sandy River welcomes the Bull Run into its flows about forty miles away from the Sandy's alpine origin—and well beyond the conduits that channel Bull Run water into Portland—does water directly from Mount Hood mix with that of Bull Run.

But Mount Hood cannot be viewed in isolation. Its impacts and influence spread far beyond the 11,239-foot mass that rises from some set-in-volcanic-stone geographical coordinates along the spine of the Cascade Range. What Portlanders see of Hood from the city is but a fraction of the actual peak, most of which unfolds in the forests below. The mountain and its predecessors helped sculpt the very landscape of the Pacific Northwest. A landslide of leftover volcanic debris is believed to have dammed off Bull Run Lake itself 10,000 years ago. Tens of thousands of years earlier, volcanic flows and deposits from Hood and other Cascadian vents laid the groundwork for the porous basin that now underlies the lake. There's also a possibility, albeit a remote one, that a small amount of groundwater from Mount Hood might eventually seep its way into the Bull Run watershed. Hood itself is the most prominent manifestation of exactly why the Bull Run watershed gets so much rainfall; the mountain, and more importantly the lesser ridge of volcanic peaks that came before it and now serve as its foothills, push marine air up and over the range, causing it to let loose its moisture in buckets.

And perhaps most importantly in relation to Bull Run, Mount Hood poses one of the most substantial threats to the entire watershed and the drinking water for nearly a million Oregonians. A volcanic eruption on Hood could send massive landslides, debris flows, and ash into the watershed, rendering the water turbid beyond use since, at present anyway, Bull Run water is not filtered. In fact, ash from the 1980 eruptions of Mount St. Helens rained into the Bull Run watershed, raising concerns at the water bureau. Eruptions could also trigger lahars that could damage any of the aboveground portions of the conduits that carry water from Bull Run to Portland. Such concerns in part led the water bureau on a $21 million project in 2009 to reroute two major conduits from a bridge across the Sandy River near Dodge Park into a 400-foot-long tunnel 85 feet underneath the river.

So Mount Hood may not be directly responsible for or related to Portland's water supply. But like the reflection it casts in Bull Run Lake on calm, clear days, its presence and influence cannot be ignored. Almost like the sun or the wind or the high clouds, Mount Hood helps shape the lives of Oregonians in ways not often seen from off in the distance.

I CLIMBED ON THE WATER bureau's bus one sunny July morning to find it filled to the brim with twenty-five other people. A family of four next to me had thought the trip sounded like a fun summer excursion (again, only in Portland). A high-powered CEO behind me was along for civic involvement, and a reporter from the *Oregonian* next to him had written about the watershed and was planning another story. A photographer from the paper was also on board, along with a few seemingly engaged citizens, some older couples, the men in veterans baseball hats, and a couple folks who almost looked like they'd gotten on the wrong bus.

Almost from the get-go, Jody Burlin began spilling gallons of information she'd accumulated in her head over the past four years as a water resources educator. We cruised east along I-84, past the Columbia South Shore Well Field near Troutdale—the backup system to the Bull Run—and learned that 60 percent of the water bureau's customers live in Portland; the other 40 percent make their homes in outlying towns like Gresham and Tigard. Average demand on the system is 85 million gallons a day, though the summer months often push it up to more than 200 million. The average Portlander uses about 62 gallons of water each day, more than 20 percent of which goes down the toilet; in contrast, every day in Las Vegas, the average citizen uses over 200 gallons.

As we headed east on US 26 toward Mount Hood, Burlin talked about the three main pipes that channel water from Bull Run into Portland almost entirely by gravity. One pipe makes its way to a 50-million-gallon underground storage reservoir on Powell Butte; a second pipe feeds the three open reservoirs on Mount Tabor, and a third runs under the Willamette River and up to a pair of open reservoirs in Washington Park in southwest Portland.

The open reservoirs became a flashpoint in 2002, when the city proposed burying or covering them to comply with Environmental Protection Agency regulations and also to safeguard against potential terrorist attacks in a post-9/11 world. As of 2010 the reservoirs were still open. Judging by the civic uproar over the potential loss of these rather scenic and, many would say, integral features—riled citizens formed the Friends of the

Reservoirs advocacy group in 2002—it's easy to imagine some sort of . . . alternate outcome when all is said and done. Either way, according to the city, all five of these open bodies of water will at least be disconnected from the water system by 2020.

᠀

AT THE QUAINT little Zigzag Mountain Store in Zigzag, we turned north up Lolo Pass Road, a winding way into the Mount Hood National Forest that leads to signature trails, campsites on the Sandy River, climbing at Frenches Dome, and in-your-face views of Hood's western profile. We then hooked left up a road I'd never traveled: Forest Service Road 10. A locked gate keeps the riffraff out, but Burlin had the key to let us pass into the Bull Run Watershed Management Unit.

We motored among towering Douglas firs and hillsides full of volcanic gray andesite—another reminder of the area's connection to the giant mountain off in the distance—some of which was used in the handsome stonework that lines the Historic Columbia River Highway out along the Columbia River. The shadow of a red-tailed hawk cruising overhead raced alongside the bus and veered off just as we rolled up to the shoreline of Bull Run Lake.

About a mile and a half long and a half-mile wide, the pristine lake is surrounded on three sides by steep, treed hillsides thick with rhododendrons, vine maples, and, in early summer, blooming bear grass. A small, pretty island rests in the northwest corner of the lake, and out over the water, which hits about 270 feet at its deepest point, a snowy Mount Hood simply towers. The absolute best view is from the front porch of one of three rustic log cabins built in 1915 to house workers building an outlet works, a small dike, and a rock and log dam that raised the lake level by about ten feet. The lake is so scenic, so inviting, that it was not hard to imagine paddling about in a canoe or plunging in for a quick swim. Prohibited, of course—all bodily contact with the water is strictly forbidden—but an inviting picture nonetheless.

Next we filed down a pleasant little trail through the forest that surrounds and protects the watershed. Though a fire is believed to have denuded the area half a millennium ago, the place reeked of old growth: soaring and fragrant hemlocks; cedars and firs; giant fungi and ferns; young, green trees sprouting up from old snags and logs. A river percolated unseen through the trees. At the end of the trail, we came to the banks of the Bull Run River. Clear as crystal and smooth in its shallow flows over green moss and rocks of red, black, and gray, the river seemed almost anticlimactic in its modesty. But think about all that it's responsible for downstream, and the Bull Run River grows grand.

BACK OUTSIDE THE BUS, just past a tree raked by a black bear, someone joked about the irony of the *Oregonian* reporter's bottle of San Pellegrino right there next to some of the purest and tastiest water in the world. We motored on, past Falls Creek Falls, and then I saw something I'd never seen near Mount Hood before: a black bear, dashing up the road in front of us. I'd seen one in Alaska's Kenai National Wildlife Refuge during a four-day backpacking trip with a good friend from Ohio, and in Tahoe Amy and I saw a mother and cub eyeballing a Dumpster from a tree near a restaurant. We also drove past a lifeless one on the side of

Highway 101 on the southern Oregon coast, an area notorious for its scrounging bear population.

But never at Mount Hood. A few deer maybe, some squirrels and newts, lots of gray jays, but definitely no bears. Either they've all managed to stay hidden, or maybe the Mount Hood National Forest's nearly five million annual visitors just have a way of squeezing them out. Maybe they've found refuge in the sealed-off Bull Run along with 250 other wildlife species, from the fabled northern spotted owl and bald eagles to cougars, coyotes, and Roosevelt elk.

Our next stop was the first of two Bull Run dams that together impound seventeen billion gallons of water. The first one, cleverly named Bull Run Dam 1, is a giant concrete and steel bow built between 1927 and 1929 that holds back ten billion gallons. If it were to ever let go, an eighty-five-foot-tall wall of water would thunder down the river and likely wipe out anything in its path, including the famous Tad's Chicken 'n Dumplins about ten miles downstream in Troutdale. We walked 250 steps down to the base of the dam and went inside, where it was damp, dripping, and cold, like a catacomb. In the middle of the passageway was an odd contraption of valves and giant padlocked chains. Opening these would be like pulling the plug from a giant bathtub drain.

DURING A BREAK at Bear Creek House, built for the construction supervisor in 1927 and overlooking Dam 1, our driver, Lauren Holwege, shared a few stories from his time in the watershed. A big, friendly guy with grayish hair and a brass belt buckle, Holwege worked for the water bureau in Bull Run for thirty-two years, including as public works manager, before retiring. Throughout the day, he recalled being spooked by five deer while working security at Bull Run Dam 1 in the 1970s and how City Commissioner Randy Leonard, who helped procure the comfortable rig for watershed tours, always favored the bus's onboard loo.

Holwege also talked about the logging trucks that used to rumble in and out of the Bull Run.

"I used to have to dodge them all day long," he said. "It was not fun coming up here then. They got paid by the trip, not by the hour, so it was no fun at all."

As for the size of some of the trees being hauled out, Holwege said, "There were times I remember seeing just one log on a truck. That was all it could carry."

After Roosevelt signed the Trespass Act in 1904, giving Portland claim to the only water rights granted to a major city by a US president, people pretty much left the Bull Run alone. The water bureau logged an area along the river in the late 1920s and built Bull Run Dam 1 to create the gigantic reservoir, but otherwise it was pretty much hands-off the Bull Run.

But after World War II, a hungry and victorious nation needed lumber for houses. Lots of lumber for lots of houses. And the US Forest Service needed money. Lots of money. And lo and behold, the Bull Run was filled with tens of thousands of acres of prime old-growth trees that could provide both. In the early 1950s, the Forest Service began to push for logging in the Bull Run. Knowing that Portlanders might not take too kindly to clear-cuts next to their drinking water, especially to enrich a timber company or government bureaucracy, the Forest Service focused its public relations not on revenue, but on the premise that logging would reduce the risk of a catastrophic fire in the watershed.

A secret memo from a ranger in 1952 making the case for timber harvests cautioned that Portlanders, who relished the idea of an unspoiled watershed, would likely raise hell if logging were allowed in the Bull Run.

"There is a tremendous P.R. job to change this thinking of some 50 years standing," the memo said. "The fire angle should be played up and revenue returns subdued in this initial discussion."

The approach worked, initially, and by 1958 loggers were wiping away swaths of old-growth trees inside the watershed. Because the work was done on the down-low, not many people knew about it. Anyone who raised questions was assured that the operations were small and targeted toward fire control. Newspaper photos showed horses wearing diapers—supposed proof of the operation's commitment to cleanliness—as they hauled trees out of the watershed. In reality, the major extraction was all mechanized, and by 1972 nearly 16 percent of the watershed had been logged or impacted by logging. Three hundred miles of roads had been plowed through the Bull Run, and according to an article in *American Scientist* by Douglas Larson, a scientist who served on the Bull Run Advisory Committee in the late 1970s, the Forest Service had plans to log half of the Bull Run by 2000. Images from a 2009 Oregon Public Broadcasting segment on the watershed show extensive clear-cuts nearly within a stone's throw of one reservoir; other aerial images show a patchwork of extraction across the Bull Run.

Fortunately for those who wanted to preserve the Bull Run, many of the logging trucks rumbled back and forth through the community of Marmot west of Mount Hood and near the weekend cabin of Portland physician Joseph Miller. Curious about the logging trucks at first, and then dissatisfied with the answers he got from the water bureau and the Forest Service, Miller started digging around to find out just what was going on in the Bull Run. He sued the Forest Service in 1973 for violating the Trespass Act, and even though the Forest Service fought, saying loggers weren't trespassers since they'd been given permission to enter the watershed, a federal judge in 1976 ruled in favor of Miller.

Just a year later, however, Oregon congressmen Mark Hatfield and Robert Duncan sponsored legislation signed by President Jimmy Carter that not only shrunk the boundary of the management unit, but that also allowed the Forest Service to continue logging in Bull Run so long as it did not impact water quality. Miller and several environmental groups continued the battle for years. In 1983 a massive windstorm blew down nearly 6,000 acres of old-growth timber in the Bull Run, nearly all of it adjacent to huge clear-cuts and logging roads. Despite opposition, the Forest Service began salvage logging of that timber in 1988.

ON A TYPICAL SPRING Oregon day in 1991, rainy, gray, and green, Regna Merritt, executive director of the environmental group Oregon Wild from 2000 to 2010, accompanied Joseph Miller and a handful of other activists to a gated road in the Mount Hood National Forest inside Bull Run. They were there to protest the Olive timber sale, an area inside the management unit that had just weeks prior been identified as critical habitat for the spotted owl.

Merritt, whose mother, Justine, had headed a 1985 effort to encircle the Pentagon with miles of handmade fabric panels to mark the fortieth anniversary of the nuclear bombing of Hiroshima and Nagasaki, had found in Miller a kindred spirit.

"He was the inspiration for me getting involved in that work," she said.

Merritt made sure that the media turned out to capture whatever was to transpire on that soggy May morning.

Decked out in a down coat, rain hat, and round eyeglasses, Miller, by then in his eighties, stood in front of the gate while people a quarter of his age—Merritt's five-year-old daughter was there, too—clapped and danced to a jig played by a longhair on the fiddle. Protesters had locked the gate with a bicycle U-lock, but Forest Service officials and Clackamas County Sheriff's deputies gave loggers the go-ahead to open it and start cutting. The loggers attached a cable to the lock and sprung it off into the woods like a five-pound metal boomerang.

"Are you crazy?" someone yelled.

With the gate open and the trucks gearing up to head in, Miller shuffled past the deputies and sprawled out in the middle of the road. His cohorts followed suit, locking arms and leaving the authorities utterly confounded. They ordered the group to get up or face arrest. Nobody moved. So three deputies picked Miller up off the ground and carted the octogenarian off like a side of beef. He was later escorted away with his hands cuffed over his white-haired head to be charged and ultimately convicted of disorderly conduct.

"I've got your hat and your dog, Joe," one of the deputies said as the others spirited him away. "Don't worry."

Despite Miller's protest, the trees in the Olive sale met their maker through the teeth of a chainsaw.

But the good doctor's continued efforts did eventually pay off. In the winter of 1996, massive rains inundated Oregon, and rain-on-snow events unleashed huge volumes of water that pushed streams and rivers out of their banks. The Willamette River, which runs through the very heart of Portland, rose some thirty feet and nearly topped the downtown seawall that corrals the river through town. Out in the Bull Run, especially as a result of clear-cut logging, so much soil and debris clogged the watershed that the city of Portland had to shut down the water system—for the first time ever—and draw water from the backup Columbia South Shore Well Field for eight days.

Shortly thereafter, Senator Mark Hatfield, whose 1977 legislation had helped reopen the Bull Run to logging, successfully introduced the Oregon Resources Conservation Act, which prohibited any more logging in the watershed. And in 2001 Congress passed the Little Sandy Protection Act, further protecting the Bull Run and expanding the boundaries of the management unit to include most of the Little Sandy River watershed, which sits just to the southwest of the Bull Run.

Miller, who had donated all but two and a half of his ninety-four acres in Marmot to the Audubon Society of Portland, helped push both acts of legislation and lived to see them come to fruition. He died in 2007 at the age of ninety-six.

WEATHER

I wield the flail of the lashing hail,
And whiten the green plains under,
And then again I dissolve it in rain,
And laugh as I pass in thunder.

—Percy Bysshe Shelley, "The Cloud"

There is nothing like a beautiful early spring day on the mountain. Sunshine like it's the beach, blue sky clear as a bell, and the snow white and pure. A study in colorful definitions.

With the summit positively shining in the high distance, my friend Darin May and I set off on a conditioning hike to Illumination Rock, a massive basalt outcrop at 9,543 feet on Mount Hood. An absolutely enthusiastic mountain man—he once ran up the 10,300-foot South Sister in an evening, then summited again early the next morning with the rest of us mere mortals who'd camped on a lower plateau at the edge of the tree line—Darin is an exciting guy to head up a giant slope with. He shoots from the hip with every sentence through a stutter that only heightens the impact of his delivery. He loves Jack London and cracks me up with obscenity-laden tales from his days on an Alaskan fishing boat.

We trudged up the Palmer Snowfield while seemingly everyone else was making their way down. Skiers and boarders skimmed by, and worn out climbers dropped one heavy foot in front of the other on their way back to the parking lot after a long, long night. One came glissading down through the slush and ran out of gas at our feet: Trin, a friend from the Ptarmigans, a mountaineering club in Vancouver, just cruising back from a solo trip to the summit. That's one of the many beauties of Mount Hood. There are times, camped high up above Vista Ridge on the northwest side, for example, when you feel solitude so wild that you forget a major metropolitan mess of more than 2 million people is little more than an hour's drive west. On other days, you run into familiar faces on the slopes as if you were just crossing paths at a coffee shop in town.

By the time Darin and I were halfway up the Palmer, the clouds had begun to roll in. At first they just peppered the blue sky, but the higher up we got, the more they stitched themselves into a patchwork of white and gray. The wind picked up on cue, swirling the first few snowflakes around like downy feathers. We crested the Palmer, bedecked now in all our worst-case-scenario gear: gloves and hats, shells and ski goggles. I never thought I'd be putting any of that on that day, but there we were.

With the winds whipping enough to force us into a yelling conversation, crazy Darin decided it was high time he practiced his snow cave skills. He shoveled around a bit, then for some reason took off a glove—and couldn't get it back on. By then, it was bitter cold and the wind and snow were howling enough to knock us off balance. Visibility was suddenly laughable, twenty feet at best.

Darin started swearing in a booming voice about his glove while I tried my best to help him tug it down over bright red fingers. Even though we were less than two hours uphill from Timberline, I started to get seriously nervous about how this might turn out. Wasn't it a sunny, summery day just a minute ago?

Luckily it's easy to follow the Palmer lift and then the Magic Mile lift all the way back down to Timberline in a whiteout, especially with the wind bowing the overhead cables like a string bass. Darin and I slogged down from tower to tower and ended up back at the lodge with, thankfully, all of his fingers and a newfound respect for the weather on Mount Hood.

MOUNTAINS DO CRAZY things to the weather.

I've been lost in the clouds for two hours on Mount Adams when, not an hour earlier, I'd been soaking in the rays on its summit. I've stood next to a best friend at the edge of a ridge in the Goat Rocks Wilderness in Washington and watched clouds pour like a river down into the valley below. I've been snowed on in August at Green Lakes near South Sister and soaked by a twenty-four-hour Columbia River Gorge deluge in June.

Welcome to the Northwest.

"The Cascades are a huge driver as to our weather in western Oregon in general," said Matt Zaffino, chief meteorologist at Portland TV station KGW. "They make my job a lot of fun."

An avid outdoorsman himself—when I met him to talk Mount Hood weather he'd just finished a physical therapy session for a ski injury he sustained while covering the 2010 Winter Olympics in Vancouver, British Columbia—Zaffino is probably

Portland's most-recognizable weatherman. He looks the part of an active Northwesterner and has a trademark voice that turned heads in recognition at the tables around us. Zaffino is also the only forecaster who's ever done a live weather broadcast from the summit of Mount Hood. Granted, the weather balloon he launched from up there immediately sank like a stone down the north side, but it was still a first and only.

Weather in the Pacific Northwest and, more specifically, Western Oregon, is largely influenced by terrain: the Coast Range mountains, the Willamette Valley, the Columbia River Gorge, the hills around Portland, and, of course, the Cascades. Because of all this different terrain, there's plenty of variation in weather within short distances. Driving through the Coast Range for a day at the beach, for example, can sometimes be an exercise in wild mood swings, with the inland mountains being completely smothered in clouds and fog while the coastline, just a few miles to the west, basks in warm sun.

One of the keys to cloud formation, something in abundance here in the Northwest, is lift. And one of the primary mechanisms behind lift in these parts are mountains. The damp air that rolls in off the Pacific rises at the ridge of the Cascades, where it cools, condenses into clouds, and then lets loose in the form of rain or snow. As the air descends on the eastern side of the mountains, it warms, causing more evaporation, less precipitation, and more clear, sunny days, a.k.a. the rain shadow.

"You can see it plainly on the satellite image," Zaffino said. "The marine layer and the cloud line right up to the crest of the Cascades and then . . . clear."

Because there's so much moisture in the air in the Pacific Northwest, the Cascades are able to wrest more rain and snow from the clouds than other ranges. The average snowfall on Hood varies between 400 and 500 inches per year; in Aspen and Vail, Colorado, it's around 180 inches annually. The national, all-time record—1,140 inches or 95 feet—piled up on Mount Baker, a 10,778-foot Cascade peak north of Seattle, in 1999. With all that extra moisture, however, comes snow that is much heavier and stickier than in the Rockies. Skiers call it Cascade concrete.

JUST ABOUT EVERY FALL, Zaffino hears from someone sure that Mount Hood is erupting. But what they're usually mistaking for volcanic apocalypse is little more than the dramatic formation of lenticular clouds. The clouds, often pegged as UFOs as well, look like giant dinner plates hovering around the mountain. Though they seem like they're suspended, lenticulars are actually moving like rivers of moisture over the crest of a mountain or ridge and thus often portend changing weather. High winds drive the air up toward the mountain and at some point, depending on moisture level, the air cools enough to reach condensation and form a cloud. But once the air passes over the mountain, it starts to descend and the cloud evaporates.

"It looks like the cloud is never moving," Zaffino said, "but it's actually constantly forming on the windward side, constantly dissipating on the downward side, and the air is just continually moving through it."

Unique mountain clouds create other optical effects around Mount Hood as well. When sunrise conditions are ripe and a cloud layer forms above the mountain, an inverse shadow of the peak gets projected onto the clouds. From a distance, it actually does look like the mountain is spewing a dark cloud of ash into the sky. Climbers on Hood are also occasionally witness to a creepy phenomenon known as the *Brocken spectre*, an eerie, haloed apparition that appears when a climber's shadow is magnified and cast on clouds down below. First described in 1780 by the German scientist Johann Silberschlag, the ghostly specter takes its name from the Brocken, a 3,700-foot peak in the Harz Mountains of central Germany.

Though it might at times seem as if Mount Hood is creating its own unique weather, Zaffino said that's not usually the case. If it's happening on the mountain, he said, it's directly related to the meteorological forces swirling around the bigger picture. In addition, those surprise storms that come out of nowhere and strand climbers up on the mountain like the one Darin and I stumbled upon? Nice try, but something in the forecast more than likely provided at least a clue. Admitting that forecasters aren't always right and that sometimes weather changes happen earlier or later than expected, Zaffino nevertheless said that most major storms do tip their hands, even if it can sometimes be hard to read all the cards.

Some friends of his were camped in the sunshine at Illumination Rock one February weekend. Conditions there on Hood were fantastic, so even though some weather had been forecast to come in, they decided to give the summit a go early the next morning. What they couldn't see from their campsite on the south side of Hood, and what Zaffino saw during a run up in Portland's West Hills that same day, was some serious lenticulation going on above Rainier and Adams—a sign that change was afoot. The next morning, his friends awoke to a howling whiteout. On their way down, a rope team of three got lost, plunged into White River Canyon, and spent a frigid night on the mountain until help arrived the next day.

Those kinds of circumstances are anomalies, however. Using data collected in part from weather balloons released from Salem twice a day, meteorologists build model forecasts that are fairly accurate. Weather folks around the state, including Zaffino, who'd been working at a TV station in southern Oregon at the time, forecast with certainty the deadly storm on Hood that overtook a climbing party from Oregon Episcopal School in 1986. Same with the one that socked climbers Brian Hall, Kelly James, and Jerry Cooke on the north face in 2006. That one came at the tail end of a stretch of dry, clear December weather that the climbers, not forecasters, might have expected to last longer than it did. The storm blasted the mountain with snow, frigid temperatures, and sustained winds of more than a hundred miles an hour.

"To walk in a sustained wind of hurricane strength, which is seventy-four miles per hour, is damn near impossible, let alone a hundred," Zaffino said. "I think those guys summited and then were trying to crawl their way down the mountain, but they couldn't do it. They just physically could not do it."

TREES

A war on terror, a war on drugs
A war on kindness, a war on hugs
A war on birds and a war on bees
They got a war on hippies trying to save the trees

—Michael Franti, "We Don't Stop"

IT TAKES A LOT to stand out in Portland. Mohawks, piercings, ironic facial hair, tattoos, exotic pets, naked bicyclists, a bag-piper in a Santa Claus suit playing Christmas carols on a unicycle in Pioneer Courthouse Square—all just another day in P-town.

Even so, the person I was looking for one sunny summer day in the polished Pearl District stuck out like a weed in a bed of flowers, or vice versa. He was on a bike, a mane of wild brown curls trailing down his shoulders like a train. No shirt. No shoes. An earthy tree medallion dangling from his neck. It had to be him.

Tre Arrow.

We'd met at a coffee shop—I grabbed an iced coffee, he went for a chai with hemp milk—to talk about his rather unique connection to the Mount Hood National Forest, particularly a few groves of trees out along Eagle Creek in the peak's southwest foothills.

"Those trees out there are part of my family," he said.

Drinks in hand, we pulled up some chairs in the sunshine and Tre Arrow proceeded to tell me about the role that the towering trees of Eagle Creek played in taking him from unknown environmental activist to ledge-sitting firebrand to the FBI's Ten Most Wanted Fugitives list right alongside Osama bin Laden.

⤶

BORN MICHAEL J. SCARPATTI near Akron, Ohio, in 1974—he legally changed his name in 2000—Arrow grew up in Florida in a family that wasn't particularly politically or environmentally minded. But at Florida State University in the mid-1990s, he began learning about the contaminated Love Canal neighborhood in western New York and the toxic pollution that Procter & Gamble had been dumping into the Fenholloway River in Florida. Inspired, Arrow got involved in some campus activism, sold his truck, and started evolving his diet into one that focused around raw foods and vegetarianism. He headed west in 1996, and in 1998 he and the rest of the country got to know Julia Butterfly Hill, the environmental activist who lived in a 1,500-year-old redwood tree in northern California for two years to keep the Pacific Lumber Company from cutting it down.

"When I heard about her, I thought, wow, that's what I want to do," Arrow said. "I wanted to do something more direct-action oriented."

As fate would have it, Arrow arrived in Portland for a raw food festival in 2000, and by then, protesters had been hanging out in the trees above Eagle Creek for close to two years.

THE MILLION-ACRE Mount Hood National Forest, known until 1924 as the Oregon National Forest, is home not only to Oregon's signature peak, but to everything from lakes, rivers, and natural hot springs to historic lodges and rustic cabins, a thousand miles of hiking trails, more than eighty campgrounds, and a handful of unique climbing crags. Although few and far between, bears live in the forest, as do cougars. Amy and I heard a female cougar scream one dark night; it was the most blood-chilling sound I've ever heard. Deer, elk, coyotes, pocket gophers, marmots, elusive wolverines, and hundreds of other wildlife species also call the forest home. So do bald eagles and ospreys, northern spotted owls, bobbing American dippers, downy woodpeckers, and rufous hummingbirds. Some summers, migrating California tortoiseshell butterflies swarm by the millions across the forest as they make their way along the Cascades—a surreal phenomenon I found myself surrounded by on the top of the 10,000-foot Middle Sister one summer.

Throughout the forest there are mushrooms—shiitakes, morels, chanterelles—ferns, wild herbs, huckleberries and salmonberries, lichen like old-man's beard and witch's hair, and sprawling meadows of wildflowers: the spring-heralding trillium; foxgloves, tall and decked with pink and purple flowers and the source of digitalin, a medicinal agent used to treat irregular heartbeats; bear grass, the long blades of which Native Americans wove into watertight baskets; the western anemone, an unremarkable white flower in bloom that grows a shaggy, Muppet-like head after the petals fall off.

The Mount Hood National Forest is also, naturally, host to trees. Lots of trees—some of which are the biggest conifers in the world. Giant trees like the Douglas fir, named after the Scottish botanist David Douglas, who mislabeled the tree as a pine; western red cedars; noble firs; and the towering ponderosas of the east side. Smaller trees like western hemlocks, white pines, bigleaf and vine maples, the black cottonwood. Subalpine trees—firs and the rare whitebark pine—stunted by snowpack and frigid winds into haggard, bony fingers called *krummholz*, fifty years older than their diminutive height betrays.

Trees, too, that make some of the best two-by-fours on the market.

Across the Northwest, timber long reigned as king. The region's seemingly endless waves of old-growth firs and cedars drew timber barons from the east—Frederick Weyerhaeuser, for one—who by the beginning of the twentieth century had made quick work of the hardwood forests of the East Coast and the Midwest.

For decades in the forests surrounding Mount Hood, trees fell like dominoes, fuelling area sawmills, providing lumber for housing and construction, revenue for logging companies, and jobs for loggers and millworkers in towns like Estacada, Boring, Sandy, and Hood River. In the early 1920s loggers were harvesting about 25 million board feet of timber from the Mount Hood National Forest every year. By the late 1940s the annual harvest was up to roughly 150 million board feet, and in both 1965 and 1977 nearly 500 million board feet of timber came out of the forest—enough to frame more than 34,000 average 2,000-square-foot houses.

But in the 1980s mechanization, economic declines, and changing public sentiment began to hack away at the Northwest timber industry. Harvest levels around Mount Hood swung wildly, from less than 200 million board feet in 1983 back up to more than 400 million in 1989.

"For a remarkable amount of time, close to forty years even, there was agreement among the government and the citizenry that an important role of National Forest lands was to provide timber," said Gary Larsen, supervisor of the Mount Hood National Forest through 2010. "But then we entered a time when the importance of timber no longer was uncontested. People realized that the only remaining old growth in the US was left on public lands, and the level of timber production we had didn't fit well with preserving the legacy of old growth for future generations."

In 1990 the northern spotted owl joined the list of threatened animals that are protected under the Endangered Species Act, a move that all but froze the saw blades when it came to trees in the National Forest. Throughout the 1990s, logging in the Mount Hood National Forest dropped precipitously. President Clinton's Northwest Forest Plan, implemented as a kind of compromise in 1994, set the harvest levels for the forest at 64 million board feet—300 million less than it had been up to that point.

Though the plan locked up much of the state's remaining old-growth timber, in 1995 a notorious caveat known as the salvage rider rendered a range of controversial timber sales exempt from environmental regulations.

"It was logging without laws," said Alex P. Brown, executive director of Bark, an environmental organization dedicated to protecting and preserving the Mount Hood National Forest.

One group of salvage rider sales concerned 28 million board feet of timber in the Mount Hood National Forest from century-old trees towering above a crystalline stream southwest of Mount Hood. That stream: Eagle Creek.

ACTIVISTS DIDN'T WANT the trees around Eagle Creek to be cut. Spread out over about a thousand acres, the trees are huge but not really old growth, as a fire swept through and cleared the area about 150 years ago. But because the acres have never been logged, they are in pristine condition. They butt up against the Salmon-Huckleberry Wilderness in the Mount Hood National Forest and, at the time, environmental groups like the Oregon Natural Resources Council (ONRC) and the Cascadia Forest Alliance (CFA) singled out Eagle Creek as an ideal future addition to the forest's stock of designated wilderness. They also pointed out that Eagle Creek was within the Clackamas River watershed, which provides clean drinking water to close to 200,000 people. Damage to the trees and streams in the watershed would impact anyone drinking the water as well. Two years after the timber had been sold to Vanport Manufacturing for just over $10 million, even the owner of the company, Adolf Hertrich, was open to exchanging the trees for something a little less controversial.

But the Forest Service pressed on, and because Eagle Creek had been sold under the salvage rider, activists had little to no recourse in the courtroom.

"The only way people could have any input was to get out in the streets and actually take direct action," said Brown, who at the time worked as a volunteer for both CFA and ONRC.

For Eagle Creek, that meant roadblocks and wooden platforms high up in the trees occupied by at least one activist at all times. Forest advocates also built several pods above the Forest Service roads into the timber sale area. Some of the pods were built in such a way that any attempt to remove them, either by dismantling them or cutting support lines, could send the activist inside plunging to the ground sixty feet below.

By the summer of 2000 tensions had begun to boil at Eagle Creek. The Forest Service was ready to get on with it, but the activists, including by then Tre Arrow, weren't giving an inch. In July the tree sitters were running low on supplies and support, so Arrow and a few others left the forest and went back into Portland to drum up reinforcements. A couple days later, armed Forest Service personnel—known to the activists as the freddies—raided and cleared the camps. During the operation, seventeen-year-old Emma Murphy-Ellis, an activist in one of the pods who went by the name *Usnea*—the scientific name for old-man's beard lichen—cinched a noose around her neck, bike-locked it to the main traverse line, and proceeded to cut five of the six lines supporting the pod as agents approached. One more line cut and she would have hanged herself high above the Forest Service road. She acquiesced more than ten hours later only at the pleading of her fellow activists.

Steamed that he'd been in the city and not among the trees during the raid, Arrow was raring to go for a rally CFA had planned in front of the Forest Service's headquarters in the Robert Duncan Plaza in downtown Portland that evening at six o'clock. People started gathering in front of the tan brick building as scheduled, but there weren't many workers left in the Forest Service office. Arrow felt like something else needed to happen to really grab attention and keep the people interested. That's when he noticed a perfect set of brick handholds running up the side of the building to a ledge about thirty feet up.

"The way they built that building, they just wanted somebody to climb it," said Arrow, who'd honed his climbing chops at places like Yosemite and Idaho's City of Rocks. "So I did."

In front of crowd and camera, Arrow free-climbed up the side of the building to the nine-inch ledge, instantly bringing Eagle Creek and the Mount Hood National Forest into downtown Portland.

"Sometimes Tre has poor impulse control," said Donald Fontenot, a key organizer and spokesman with CFA at the time, "but the wall sit was genius."

Over the next eleven days, Arrow lived on the ledge, rallying the troops with a bullhorn, hanging signs, taking care of his business in a bucket. A fellow activist built him a platform that attached to the ledge with a C-clamp anchor system. The Forest Service taped trespassing warrants on the windows behind him. He conducted countless interviews via cell phone and otherwise kept Eagle Creek front and center in the public eye for nearly two weeks.

When he felt he'd made his point—and after he'd worked out a lenient agreement for the trespassing charge—Arrow came down.

It would take nearly two more years—during which time the tree sits continued—but in April of 2002, the Forest Service at last cancelled the Eagle Creek timber sale, citing a scientific review that showed that logging could be detrimental to adjacent stands and the watershed. About 40 percent of the original acreage had been cut.

Just days after the agency cancelled the sale, twenty-two-year-old activist Beth O'Brien died after falling more than a hundred feet while climbing up one of the Eagle Creek trees without a safety harness.

❧

AFTER EAGLE, Arrow himself took a fall. In the general election of 2000, he unsuccessfully ran for Congress, garnering 15,000 votes as a candidate of the Green Party. In October of 2001, while protesting another timber sale in an area of Oregon's Tillamook State Forest known as Gods Valley, Arrow fell close to eighty feet from a hemlock tree after law enforcement officers and loggers chased him through the trees and deprived him of sleep for more than two days. He ended up with a collapsed lung, a fractured pelvis, a dislocated shoulder, and a concussion, but he was alive.

But Tre took an even bigger fall in August 2002, when the FBI indicted him and three others for firebombing trucks at Ross Island Sand and Gravel Co. in Portland and two logging trucks and a front-end loader at Ray A. Schoppert Logging, one of the companies contracted to cut at Eagle Creek. The incidents caused close to $300,000 in damage and led some sawmills to cancel orders for timber from Eagle Creek. The three others accused of participating in the 2001 crimes were caught, pleaded guilty while implicating Arrow, and served prison terms of up to three and a half years. But Arrow took off and laid low in Canada—during which time he earned a spot on the FBI's most-wanted list—until he tripped up in 2004 trying to shoplift a pair of bolt cutters from a home improvement store. He fought extradition but eventually, after more than four years in detention in Canada, was brought back to Oregon. Faced with a potential life sentence, Arrow pleaded guilty to two arson charges even though he's always maintained his innocence and tagged the FBI's case against him as politically motivated. He was sentenced to six and a half years in prison, including time served in Canada. By December 2009, he was again a free man.

SITTING ACROSS FROM Tre Arrow outside the coffee shop that 2010 summer afternoon, people turning their heads to see what the long-haired, shirtless, shoeless guy was cackling about, I had hoped to get all the way to the end of his story. It's a fascinating one and, to be sure, a multisided one. When I mentioned to people that I was going to talk to him, some smiled and remembered him up on the ledge ten years earlier; others shook their heads or rolled their eyes. When Arrow had been caught in 2004, Lyle Schoppert, then-president of the logging company that had lost $50,000 in equipment from the 2001 arsons, told the *Oregonian* that the world was a safer place with Tre Arrow behind bars. After a night spent talking with Donald Fontenot, the former spokesman for

CFA, he told me he wasn't sure if Tre had done what he'd pleaded guilty to; he'd never asked.

I never asked Tre Arrow if he'd done it either. After a couple hours of conversation, we both had to leave, and despite some efforts to get back together, we never did. I ran into him at the Pickathon music festival later that summer. He was volunteering in a geodesic dome that City Repair, a community organization in Portland, had built in the woods. He gave me and my family huge hugs, and when we saw him walking the grounds later on, barefoot and shirtless, he was passing out organic vegetables to anyone who would take one, including my four-year-old, Madeline, who snagged a dirty carrot from his hands.

"A little dirt never hurt," he said. Madeline laughed and ran on.

I don't know if Tre Arrow had any hand in what happened with those logging and gravel trucks. I know that he pleaded guilty and that he also did some real time. But I also remember him up on that ledge. And I do know that most of those trees out along Eagle Creek are still there. They became part of the federally designated Salmon-Huckleberry Wilderness in the Mount Hood National Forest in 2009.

FALL

MORNING SUNSHINE THROUGH *the tent walls here on the Sandy River. It's cool and comfortable in the sleeping bag, and the swishing tumble of the river just outside makes for perfect early-morning sleep. The first rays are warm enough to hint at the beautiful summer day ahead. This, and not what we swam through yesterday, is August in Oregon.*

Ramona Falls dazzles, just as I thought it would, and we stop to filter our water from its pools. Then it's in and out along the trail, past gargantuan firs and cedars, crossing the three channels of the Muddy Fork of the Sandy River, and laying eyes upon high-up water-falls, a view that only a stout pair of hiking legs can deliver. Though it's thinly veiled this morning behind patchy clouds, Hood up here, where we've never been before and with no one else around, no civilization in sight, feels primal and prehistoric.

We traipse on, find a spur trail over Bald Mountain, and tread again on familiar ground on our way up to McNeil Point, a popular and scenic rise named for outdoorsman and Oregon Journal writer Fred McNeil. Something about the slog up this forested ridge always has a way of draining the juice right out of both Amy and me every time we come up here. It's not that bad, really, just 1,500 feet or so over a couple miles, but it seems worse than that. Mosquitoes, sweat, overloaded packs. Whatever. It's unusually tiring every time.

This time, seven miles into day two of our circuit, is no different. An old hip injury of Amy's has come back to haunt her, as have a few blisters and we have no moleskin. Me, I'm feeling my knees more than I should, but I'm also carrying more in my pack than I should. No bugs this time, though. We pass a couple women on their way down and Oliver greets one with a muddy paw to the midsection. He bounds off with a grin, leaving me there to make amends. I smile and offer a useless apology. The woman is not amused. Oliver is long gone, like someone who's cut and run on his dinner check.

Through the thinning trees higher up, the mountain's silhouette rises and reveals itself just enough to entice. From here, halfway up the mountain's flanks, Mount Hood's signature face is an ideal mountain writ large. You can see cracks in the jumbled Sandy Glacier and hear the shushing headwaters of the Muddy Fork down below, follow the serrated lines of Yocum and Cathedral Ridges, peer all the way up to the true summit. From up here, approaching 6,000 feet, you really start to get a sense that you are up on the mountain, not simply close to it.

We finally crest the ridge and follow the flattening trail as it wends around a few open meadows and seasonal ponds. Orange paintbrush, white bear grass, purple lupine. Relief. Most of our elevation for the day is behind us, so it's practically a walk in the park from here to our camp for the night over in Cairn Basin.

Except right then, Amy falls.

Her boot thuds on the trail just as we're approaching a happy, outdoorsy couple, and she stumbles forward, careening face-first toward the ground. Her poles sprawl, her pack pitches, and down she goes. Not what we need right now. Her hip's been aching all day, her blisters burning, and then that familiar old trudge up here has worked its magic yet again. A pack of Nutter Butters jettisons from a side pocket. Oliver freaks and starts bounding and barking in alarm, like everyone from here to the coast just has to know we've got someone down. I bawl at him, not thinking for an instant that doing so here, in the middle of all this beauty and peace, is not only entirely inappropriate but probably makes me look and sound just a tad too close to the edge.

The happy couple, now uncomfortable, walks away.

No worries. It's best if we just put this back together on our own, which we do. I wipe the dirt off Amy's forehead, help her right herself, pick up the Nutter Butters (a campsite delicacy), and we move on toward Cairn Basin, leaving a return trip up to the stone shelter at McNeil Point for some other grueling day.

TIMBERLINE

Timberline Lodge is, itself, a mountain in miniature.

—Leverett G. Richards

THERE IS A CLASSIC LOOP tour in northwest Oregon that anyone who lives anywhere near Portland, moves to the city, or who visits friends or family that live here, is nearly required to experience if they are to get a true overview of just how fabulous this little corner of the world is.

It heads east out of the Rose City on Interstate 84, cruises through the Columbia River Gorge and all of its waterfall glory—optional stop at Multnomah Falls, the second-highest year-round waterfall in the country—and slows just enough at Hood River for lunch or at least a glimpse of the kiteboarders and windsurfers out in the river. From there it turns south on Highway 35 through the orchards of the Hood River Valley, which is hopefully backed by a massive view of Mount Hood's north face and, in the rearview mirror, Mount Adams. If the weather's nice and the mountain exceptionally beautiful, there are stops along the shoulder near the community of Mount Hood for photos.

On around the mountain, insane views of Hood and Jefferson included, the tour catches Highway 26 west and then makes a crucial right turn at the Timberline Highway. Veterans of the tour may opt for a slower and more scenic trip via the original old West Leg Road, but the main route is sufficient enough to awe. It winds its way nearly six miles up the southern base of Mount Hood, breaks out of the trees, and drops jaws wide with a huge look at the upper 5,200 feet of the mountain, all the way to its snowy white summit.

And sitting right there, literally in the shadow of Mount Hood, the one man-made wonder on this entire, requisite loop that simply cannot be missed: Timberline Lodge.

※

HAND-BUILT AS PART of Roosevelt's Works Progress Administration (WPA) in just fifteen months between 1936 and 1937, Timberline Lodge today is 55,000 square feet of idyllic mountain charm, artisan craftsmanship, and inviting, historical ambiance at 6,000 feet. Designed in a rustic and Cascadian style to mimic the mountain's peak and trailing shoulders, it is also six towering fir columns in the head house, hand-hewn over just two weeks by local cabin builder Henry Steiner for 25 dollars each. It is tons of local volcanic stone laid by Italian stonemasons, including a 92-foot-tall, 800,000-pound main chimney capped with a 750-pound brass and bronze weather vane mimicking the Wild Goose

Moon symbol from a Camp Fire Girl handbook. Fred Nobel, a professional radio tower climber, free-climbed this marvelous and dominating tower of stonework in 1938. Not surprisingly, the lodge no longer permits such daredevilry.

Timberline is fireplace andirons made from railroad rails and fireplace screens that once served as tire chains on the trucks that hauled workers building the lodge up from Government Camp. It is telephone poles turned newel posts with their tops carved into pelicans and black bears; unique oils and watercolors, lithographs and wood marquetry; intricate ironwork; holdover, hand-hooked rugs made from old blankets and worker uniforms; and chunky, carved furniture, including an armchair made specifically for Franklin Delano Roosevelt, who dedicated the lodge in 1937. It was during this dedication that George Henderson, a photographer and reporter for the *Oregon Journal*, took a photo of FDR being helped from his car. Unbeknownst to Henderson, the press was prohibited from photographing the president in any way that would show his polio-related disability. Now framed and hung on a lodge wall, it is one of the only such shots in existence.

Timberline Lodge is also seventy guest rooms, an outdoor swimming pool and amphitheater, the Ram's Head Bar, Cascade Dining Room, and the hidden little Blue Ox Bar, where Neil Young once strolled in for a serenade. The lodge helped groom the way for Oregon's ski industry, it serves as the beacon for thousands of climbers—at least in good weather—and also as the starting point for Hood to Coast, the longest relay race in the country. It is a National Historic Landmark that attracts nearly two million visitors each year. Not counting Native American casinos, it is second on the list of most-visited tourist sites in the state behind the Gorge's Multnomah Falls.

Timberline Lodge is an Oregon icon.

There was a time, though, less than twenty years after its completion, when the Forest Service thought about burning the whole thing to the ground.

RUNNING A SUCCESSFUL business at 6,000 feet on the side of a mountain wasn't easy when Timberline Lodge opened its doors in February 1938. It still isn't today, but back then, a Great Depression, a world war, and a populace not yet turned on to alpine skiing didn't help grease the skids at all. Despite a booming first season and the addition of the Magic Mile ski lift in 1939, operators of Timberline Lodge—the building has always been publicly owned but run by private entities through special-use permits—struggled. By 1942, with World War II and gas rationing in full swing, the lodge couldn't make it pencil out. Operators closed it just before the fall ski season.

At the end of the war Timberline opened again, but success remained out of reach for a handful of different operators that gave it a go. By the early 1950s the Forest Service had uncovered illicit gambling and liquor operations, including a bar and blackjack table in room 301 and slot machines on the mezzanine. Ladies of the night were rumored to be frequenting the lodge. The failure and folly of the Skiway, an aerial tram system featuring a modified city bus puttering up from Government Camp to Timberline, didn't help much either, even though the lodge had no direct involvement with it.

By January of 1955 things had gotten so bad that the Forest Service cancelled the permit of then-operator Timberline Lodge,

Inc., and the Sandy Electric Cooperative shut off the power for unpaid bills. Guests still in the lodge checked out by candlelight.

For the Forest Service, Timberline Lodge had become the big white elephant up on the big white mountain.

"Their culture at that time was cutting trees and building roads, and so Timberline was just sort of this problem," said Jeff Kohnstamm, president of RLK and Company, the entity that has run the lodge since 1955. "By then, one of the options was just burning it down."

Luckily for the lodge and the millions of visitors who've partaken of its singularity over the past fifty-six years, Kohnstamm's father, Richard, a social worker from New York with a penchant for Norwegian sweaters, had the foresight, energy, luck, and financial wherewithal from his family's success in the dye industry to try his hand at mountain resort revival. A Portland transplant as of the early 1950s, he'd also fallen for the great castles of Europe and seen how they'd become national treasures. Similarly smitten by Timberline, Kohnstamm thought the lodge might one day achieve the same kind of reverence here.

"I think him being a social worker was kind of fortuitous, because people who had any sort of business experience wouldn't have taken it on," said the younger Kohnstamm. "They would have been too smart to do that."

❦

BY THE TIME twenty-nine-year-old Richard Kohnstamm—
R. L. to longtime associates, Mr. K to employees—beat out
nearly 150 other applicants for the Timberline permit in 1955,
alpine skiing had already begun to gain popularity. Better cars
allowed people to vacation in the winter just as they had been
doing in the summer, and World War II veterans from the
Army's 10th Mountain Division, who'd become crack skiers in
Italy's Apennine Mountains, helped fuel the stateside demand
for recreational skiing at burgeoning resorts across the country,
including Timberline. The first ski school instructor R. L. hired
at Timberline Lodge, an Austrian skier from the Tyrolean Alps
named Pepi Gabl, had also sharpened his skiing skills during the
war, fighting for the Axis against Americans like Kohnstamm, a
gunner who'd been part of the force occupying Munich once the
shots had ceased.

Over the next fifty-plus years, and despite the shredded
draperies, stolen furniture, and trashed Magic Mile he walked
in on during his first day as manager, Kohnstamm the elder, his
team of collaborators, and his deep pockets helped restore and
glorify Timberline Lodge. He helped form the nonprofit Friends
of Timberline and invested heavily in the lodge and the ski area.
He installed a new Magic Mile lift, west of the original, in 1962,
and tacked on the Palmer chairlift in 1978, adding another 2,500
vertical feet to the area's highest runs. He put in a swimming pool
and also built Timberline's Wy'East Day Lodge in 1981, a building designed purposely—and, some might say, successfully—to
not compete with the grandeur of Timberline.

In the 1970s a massive and ongoing restoration project
guided by the Friends of Timberline to bring back to life or
replicate many of the original artisan features of the lodge com-
menced. Weavers and seamstresses, like Linny Adamson, who's
been Timberline's curator since 1979, tackled rugs and draperies;
woodworkers and contractors built new furniture; and black-
smiths like Russell Maugans and Darryl Nelson beefed up the
ironwork, doubling the amount that was originally in the lodge.

I ran into Nelson one day up near the lodge during
Blacksmith Week, an annual showcase of metalwork held at the
Arts Cabins in Government Camp. With his bushy moustache
and brown fedora, he fit the part of an old-school blacksmith,
and the work he's been creating for Timberline for more than
two decades looks like it's been there since day one. He makes the
frequently stolen ram's head fire pokers for guest rooms, and he's
continually upgraded door handles and hardware to keep up with
evolving fire and disability codes.

"As far as finding work, the fire marshal has helped me out
a lot," Nelson said.

In the late 1980s, Nelson and Maugans were installing
brand new twisted pine cone handrails on the main staircase
when a passing guest said, *Wow, they just don't make stuff like
that anymore.* Maugans didn't let on that the ironwork was newly
crafted.

"I asked Russell why he didn't tell the guy the truth,"
Nelson said. "And he says, 'That guy just gave us the biggest com-
pliment we could ever hope for.'"

It was also Kohnstamm who rekindled the Saint Bernard
as Timberline's mascot. A pair of the huge hounds, Lady and
Bruel, moved into the lodge in 1937 and even went on to climb to

the summit of Mount Hood a few times. Though it was never a
problem for Lady, the 200-pound Bruel always chickened out on
the descent and had to be rescued from the summit by ski patrol-
ler Hank Lewis three different times. After Lady and Bruel, hus-
kies became the lodge's mascot of choice, but Kohnstamm went
back to Saint Bernards in the 1960s with Heidi and Bruno. Since
then, there's always been a Heidi and/or a Bruno roaming the
lodge, though these days they live with longtime employees, not
in the lodge. In October 2010, three-year-old Bruno, who often
lolls about the gift shop in the Wy'East Day Lodge, was joined by
a new eight-week-old Heidi.

WHILE A LOT OF THIS was going on, Jeff Kohnstamm, now
almost fifty, was growing up. Before he was old enough for school,
he basically lived at Timberline Lodge year-round. His parents
had two adjoining rooms—110 and 112—and he and his brothers did what most little boys would do: they terrorized the place,
riding their tricycles around the lobby, throwing snowballs at
guests, and otherwise stirring up trouble. Kohnstamm, who as a
teenager worked odd jobs at the lodge before heading off to study
hotel management at Cornell, remembered his parents running
Timberline more as a quaint bed-and-breakfast than as the desti-
nation resort it would later become. Kohnstamm has fond memories of climbing Hood and skiing from its summit in high school,
befriending lodge guests and employees, the latter of whom used
to live on the third floor, and sipping his first legitimate beer in
the Ram's Head Bar.

He also remembered how hard his father worked to make Timberline live.

"Being a family business, the family's mood revolved around Dad's mood, and it could change dramatically depending on something as simple as the weather," he said. "Native Americans used to call Wy'east a moody spirit in their myths because of all the weather changes on the mountain. They had that just pegged."

After college and stints in the hospitality industry in Switzerland, New York, and California, Kohnstamm came back to work with his dad at Timberline in 1987, and in 1992 he took the helm. R. L., widely known as the man who saved Timberline Lodge, died in 2006 just a week after his eightieth birthday. A 125-acre stretch of wilderness, from the mountain's summit down into the Salmon and White River Canyons, bears his name as the Richard L. Kohnstamm Memorial Area.

Despite what might seem like a dream setup—beautiful and beloved mountain lodge, unlimited skiing, a family legacy— managing Timberline is not all sunglasses and autographs. Days when the weather is as stellar as the skiing, Jeff Kohnstamm walks around with his chest puffed out. I ran into him once at the Ram's Head, sipping a glass of red wine on a sunny Sunday afternoon and thought, *What a life.* But at other times, when a string of bad weather jeopardizes the season or when parents sit helplessly in the lodge waiting and hoping for good news of their lost climbers, the script changes.

"When things get difficult, there is a huge stress and burden," he said. "But I wouldn't trade it."

Kohnstamm won't have to trade it anytime soon. RLK and Company's current permit runs through 2038 and the family has no plans to sell it. Between now and then, additional parking is probably the biggest and most mundane of Timberline's concerns. On busy summer days the lodge's one thousand parking spaces fill up and visitors are turned away. Plans to alleviate the jam include everything from potential underground parking near the lodge and a new lot halfway up Timberline Highway to, possibly, the return of a Skiway-like tram system from Government Camp and some kind of overnight housing for summer ski camps. With climate change impacting the snow season, the ski area has also begun to look into making snow for its lower runs, and, as of 2010, the Forest Service was considering a proposal that would allow mountain bikers to course down resort terrain in the summer.

Whether or not a third generation of Kohnstamms will carry on the family's Timberline heritage is too early to tell. Kohnstamm's fifteen-year-old nephew spent part of the summer of 2010 picking up trash at the lodge, and though his own kids have expressed some interest, they were still young enough when they said hi to me in their dad's office one day to fancy video games and snowboarding over mountain resort management.

LIKE MORE THAN A FEW people who've worked at Timberline over the years—full- and part-time employee counts range from 225 to 600 throughout the year—Jon Tullis skied in the back door of the lodge and never left. A native of Connecticut who studied business and art history in college, Tullis had come west in the early 1980s looking for a little excitement. When he didn't find it in Portland, he headed to the mountain and got his fill. He planned on working and skiing at Timberline for just a few years.

A quarter of a century later, having done everything at the lodge from pushing a broom to catering and ski rentals before becoming public relations director, Tullis was still there.

"This place made sense to me from a historic and an aesthetic standpoint," he said.

Tullis met his wife on the mountain and raised his family nearby. During his time at Timberline, he established the lodge's Ski Host program, started an outdoor concert series, wrote and recorded an album of paeans to the mountain, and oversaw planning of new trails in the Still Creek Basin in 2007, an area that nearly doubled the resort's terrain below the tree line. Kohnstamm, who appreciates loyal employees and also the Grateful Dead, named the "Uncle Jon's Band" trail in Still Creek for Tullis.

Laid back, approachable, and much more subtle in his messaging than most PR flacks, Tullis sees Timberline Lodge as a gateway to the Mount Hood National Forest, much the way Old Faithful is to Yellowstone. Nearly half of the roughly 4.5 million annual visitors to the forest make at least a stop at the lodge. Unlike Mount Vernon or Monticello, which are essentially museums, Timberline still operates as it always has—as a ski lodge. It may be a federal offense to deface anything on or in the lodge, but its accessibility and preservation through use credo helps connect visitors with the lodge's unique and culturally significant architecture, artwork, and craftsmanship.

"We're not an off-limits museum or an exclusive resort. This is the people's place," Tullis said. "It was born out of the egalitarian ideal of the WPA and we operate it that way."

In 2009 Timberline came somewhat full circle when the federal government approved more than four million dollars in

American Recovery and Reinvestment Act stimulus funds for the lodge to replace windows, freshen up paint, restore chimneys, pave a parking lot, and bulk up the climbing register in the day lodge. In gearing up for the collective complaint against all things stimulus, *Wall Street Journal* editorial page writer Leslie Hook in January of that year bemoaned the government's seventy-year hand in Timberline. She grumbled about the money the Forest Service spends every year on maintenance—somewhere around $1.3 million, about a million of which comes not from taxpayers directly but from leasing fees paid by RLK—snipped at the hand Timberline was holding out for a slice of stimulus funds, and called the lodge "a New Deal gift that keeps on taking."

She then closed her piece by saying that Timberline Lodge was one of her favorite places in the entire world.

Certainly Timberline might not be around today if not for the private investment of R. L. Kohnstamm and his family. But without Uncle Sam's initial motivation and role, the lodge would never have been around at all. And considering all the other places taxpayer money ends up, one might suggest that a few hundred thousand dollars a year to maintain a signature, publicly owned alpine lodge, open to everyone and anyone who wants to stop by, and host to two million skiers, climbers, and mountain tourists from around the world every single year, might just qualify as a worthwhile investment.

MUCH OF THE WORK accomplished by the stimulus funds, save for maybe the climber's register and the solar panels slapped on the new gazebo sign at the base of Timberline Highway, involved projects that essentially keep Timberline Lodge looking and functioning the way it always has. The timeless quality of the lodge is part of what keeps people coming back. That, and maybe a certain horror movie.

"A month doesn't go by where I don't get a call about *The Shining*," Tullis said.

It's fairly widely known, or at least it should be by now, that nothing but a handful of exterior shots of Timberline Lodge made it into Stanley Kubrick's eerie 1980 adaptation of Stephen King's novel about a haunted ski lodge, a clairvoyant little boy, and an obsessed, alcoholic writer. During the opening credits, the camera follows the character played by Jack Nicholson on his long and scenic drive into the mountains for an interview at the Overlook Hotel. These first two and a half minutes were filmed along the Going-to-the-Sun Road in Montana's Glacier National Park. The scene then cuts to a summertime Timberline Lodge— the Overlook Hotel in the movie—backed by Mount Hood, gray and white and largely melted out. Near the end of the film, Scatman Crothers's character pilots a snowcat up a drifted road to the lodge to try and save the little boy from his homicidal father. Kubrick's crew filmed that at Timberline too, using one of the lodge's cats and maintenance men. But other than that, nothing was filmed at Timberline. Even scenes that look like the outside of Timberline were little more than massive sets and sound stages, including a full-size mockup of the lodge's exterior, at London's Elstree Studios.

Nonetheless, and for better or worse, Timberline has been forever tied to *The Shining*. Aware that some guests might specifically avoid or request room 217—haunted and tainted by scandal and suicide in King's novel—managers of Timberline asked

Kubrick to change the room number in his film. He switched it to 237, which does not exist at Timberline.

While walking up to the lodge one summer day, I overheard a visitor say, *Yeah, I guess this is where they filmed* The Shining. It's the urban myth that has caught on and will likely never fade. In the summer of 2002, thirty-million-album Canadian pop singer Avril Lavigne spent some time snowboarding at Timberline. She also talked with facilities manager Ed Richards, who apparently liked to toy with guests a bit when it came to the supernatural. He told Lavigne that the place was haunted—and she believed him.

The very next night, Lavigne appeared on *The Tonight Show with Jay Leno*. When he asked her where she'd flown in from, she told him, *Timberline Lodge, where* The Shining *was filmed.*

Was it scary? Leno asked.

Um, actually, yes. It's a little haunted there.

The singer told Leno that "the janitor" had taken Lavigne and her crew up to the lodge's west-end attic where they all got goosebumps and saw weird lights and freaky things.

The morning after the show aired, employees at the lodge ribbed Richards, not only because Lavigne had called him a janitor, but because he'd had no idea who he was talking to and he'd just helped spread the word to Leno's average nightly audience of five million people that Timberline Lodge was haunted.

As for ghosts at Timberline, Tullis has never seen anything, though he admitted that some others might be more in tune with the paranormal than he. Chilling enough is the death of Boris Sagal, a Hollywood film and TV director with credits like *The Twilight Zone* and *Alfred Hitchcock Presents*. In May 1981, after a day of aerial shots around Mount Hood for a TV miniseries called *World War III*, Sagal stepped out of a helicopter in the Timberline parking lot and accidentally walked into the spinning tail rotor.

Down below in Government Camp, the ghost of Ole Langerud, an accomplished skier and woodsman in the 1930s, reportedly frequents the third floor of the building that housed his ski shop for twenty-five years. Another local home is supposedly haunted by a man who hung himself during World War II, and the Old Welches Inn on the Salmon River in the Mount Hood foothills is said to have three spirits from a love triangle gone bad roaming its halls. Aficionados of the paranormal even gathered near Welches in the spring of 2010 for the Mount Hood Ghost Conference, a weekend of stories, investigations, and tours of the haunted side of northwest Oregon.

At Timberline Lodge, however, the creepiness will likely always stem from an image of a crazed, ax-wielding Jack Nicholson and an infamous, improvised tag: *Here's Johnny*.

HUT

Oh to live on Sugar Mountain
With the barkers and the colored balloons
You can't be twenty on Sugar Mountain
Though you're thinking that you're leaving there too soon
You're leaving there too soon

—Neil Young, "Sugar Mountain"

EVEN WITHOUT THE thick Boston accent, the projecting voice, the delivery and presence of the natural raconteur that he is—like an actor or singer who can simply take over a room—there's something unique about Steve Buchan. Short and solid and stacked with the stubby fingers of a strong climber, Buchan is, after all, probably the only person in the world who's ever claimed his legal residence—that is, actually had it on his driver's license—as Silcox Hut, 7,000 feet up the south side of Mount Hood.

"This guy's a character," Joe Schuberg, former manager of the Ram's Head Bar, told me when I walked in to meet Buchan one July day. "Bigger than Ben-Hur."

Jerry Gomes, a former Timberline employee who met his wife, Kaye, while working at the lodge in the seventies, added his own dash of color about Buchan.

"You remember Harry Truman, the guy who wouldn't leave Mount St. Helens when it blew up?" he asked. "Steve's going to be the Harry Truman of Mount Hood."

Born in Boston in the mid-1950s, Buchan grew up playing hockey but eventually migrated into the skiing world. He landed a job at Squaw Valley in Tahoe after high school and was on his way to ski and climb in Leavenworth, Washington, when he made a pit stop in Portland. While in the Rose City, he also headed up to Mount Hood and, after hanging out on the Palmer Snowfield for a day, found himself thinking that a summer in the Cascades might not be so bad.

"I instantly fell in love with the lodge," Buchan said.

He scored a job as a lift operator the next day and spent the summer living in the Alpine Campground, tucked in the trees at 5,400 feet just off the Timberline Highway. At the end of the summer, he accepted an offer to work on the nighttime snow removal crew, which included housing in the lodge—"Way better than camping," Buchan said—and then spent the next twelve years plowing snow in the winter and climbing and working so-so gigs like planting trees in the summer.

And then in 1993, Timberline asked him if he'd take on the task of running the newly restored Silcox Hut.

"It seemed like a golden opportunity," Buchan said. "And it was."

☙

NAMED FOR Ferdinand Silcox, chief of the US Forest Service from 1933 to 1939, Silcox Hut today is a charming stone and log mini-lodge above Timberline at 7,000 feet. Built by the WPA and the Civilian Conservation Corps in 1939, Silcox was the original terminus for the Magic Mile ski lift and also served as a warming shelter for skiers and climbers. But in 1962 Timberline relocated the Magic Mile and left Silcox to fend for itself.

It did not do well.

Unbelievably, the hut was allowed to deteriorate beyond use over the years. Vandals and the elements had their way with it, and the Forest Service eventually talked of—guess what?—burning Silcox to the ground rather than trying to keep on top of constant abuse and weather damage. Thankfully, concerned local alpinists Jon Dasler, Alan Pennington, and John Smolich stepped in with a plan to save and restore the building in the early 1980s. In 1985 they, along with Portland attorney Nancy Randall, formed the nonprofit Friends of Silcox Hut and began working with RLK and Timberline Lodge to save the historic hut. It was added to the National Register of Historic Places the same year. The three climbers were on a team trying to summit K2 in 1986 when Pennington and Smolich were tragically killed by an avalanche. Disheartened, Dasler, Randall, and other volunteers nonetheless vowed to carry on the work at Silcox. The ensuing renovation brought the hut back to its former glory and then some, adding a bunkroom, showers, and new ironwork—including Native American symbols in the door depicting the three climbers' quest to save Silcox—so that by 1993 its doors were again open to the public.

From the get-go, Silcox Hut sparked good reviews. During the day, Buchan would serve up soup and hot dogs with a side of Boston banter. When climbing season rolled around, the hut would stay open late at night, inviting climbers in for a respite by the huge stone hearth. Groups started reserving the hut for parties and couples began booking it for weddings. Once climbers began infringing on paying guests, however, Silcox cut back its late-night welcome and focused more on private gatherings. Groups now pay a per-person fee for the hut, which includes a ride up in a snowcat, dinner, breakfast, and some of the most amazing alpine scenery around.

Over the nearly two decades of its renaissance, Silcox has been host to a handful of celebrities, at least one rowdy party of Aussies and Kiwis who ran outside in the middle of the night—completely naked—for group photos with passing climbers, and guests who've been returning year after year. Buchan has served up Thanksgiving dinner for the same family five years running; he's seen other families every year for fifteen years and watched kids grow from awkward twelve-year-olds into college graduates.

Because of his time on the mountain, Buchan also has become the go-to person at Timberline for commercial film shoots. Everyone from Volvo to Victoria's Secret has done catalogs or commercials on Hood, and when high-altitude climber extraordinaire Ed Viesturs needed a shot of a climber peering down into a crevasse for his IMAX movie *Everest*, Buchan took him from Silcox up to the bergschrund on Hood's south side.

Approaching his thirtieth year on the mountain—number eighteen at Silcox—the fifty-six-year-old Buchan said he came to Hood at that singular time in life, when you're old enough to have nearly limitless freedom but young enough to be clear of any real responsibility. Unlike other, more transient folks attracted to the ski industry, Buchan kept himself "just responsible enough" to carve out one of the best and most unique gigs on the entire mountain while still enjoying the laid-back life of an inveterate skier and climber.

Over the past decade or so, he's been building his dream house on a little piece of property near Mosier with an amazing view of Mount Hood. He's doing it in Cascadian style and even having Darryl Nelson, the blacksmith who does all of Timberline's ironwork, do his. When he described it, it sounded a lot like Silcox Hut—which is good, because that's exactly what he's going for.

DOWN THE HILL

It's the quick turns that mean you're alive.

—MARK HELPRIN, *Winter's Tale*

IT CERTAINLY LOOKED LIKE A fantastic place for a beer: steep, peaked roof; massive stone chimney; cold skis stuck in the snow like a picket fence outside and a warm, amber glow from inside. The view to the north, out over the carved and sunken slopes below, showed off the broad expanse of Mount Hood's lower flanks, its upper regions hidden behind deep gray clouds.

Amy and I had just glided up to the historic warming hut at Skibowl, a popular ski resort not actually on Hood proper, but on a smaller set of foothills just to the south. The peaks that fall within the resort include Tom, Dick, and Harry Mountain, a name apparently chosen simply because there were three small peaks along this one ridge, no more, no less; Skibowl Peak; and Multorpor Mountain, a 4,650-foot mass that the Republican Club of Portland named in the early 1900s by mashing together the first few letters of Multnomah, Oregon, and Portland.

We'd spent the morning learning to downhill ski for the very first time (me) and refreshing skills not touched since a middle school ski trip (Amy). I've no excuse other than lameness for my downhill inexperience. I can't blame an Ohio upbringing for it, as one of the best ski resorts in the entire Buckeye State—Snow Trails—was just twenty-five minutes from my front door and I never went. I'm also ashamed to admit that I actually lived on the south shore of Lake Tahoe for seven months and, though I paddled and hiked and even started my climbing career there, never once stepped into a pair of ski boots.

Which is part of the reason we didn't have a beer at that charming little warming hut as I'd expected. The lesson was fine and by its end I felt like I'd mastered the snowplow off the tow-rope. We rode up the Lower Bowl lift, confidently scanning the seemingly mild terrain down below, then pointed our skis down-hill toward the hut. I fell within the first twenty feet. Then again in another ten. Amy sliced broad arcs across the short, kind of steep, maybe 300-foot slope between the lift and the hut. I fell again. And again.

I finally caught up with Amy outside the hut, still able to smile at the mess I'd made of the hill above and behind me. We scanned the hut longingly, but I was so sure that we'd be back up that day after a few more runs that we opted to pass and instead do what we really came here to do: ski.

We should have gone for that beer right then, because I flailed so badly all the way down the rest of the bowl that there was no way I was going back to do it all over again just so I could say I'd had a beer in that quaint little warming hut.

Instead, we drank bitter Mirror Ponds on the deck of the Beer Stube, at the very bottom of the Lower Bowl.

~~~

HEARTY SOULS were skiing around Mount Hood long before
the mountain's very first ski hill, the Summit Ski Area adjacent
to Government Camp, opened its slopes in 1927. The Langille
brothers, renowned north side climbing guides and part of a well-
known family of early settlers of Hood's north side, skied to the
mountain's first permanent resort, Cloud Cap Inn, on wooden
skis in 1890 to see how the inn had held up over an exceptionally
harsh winter. Members of the Snowshoe Club of Portland, who
built their cabin across from Cloud Cap in 1910, and guests of
the Mount Hood Lodge skied the mountain's northern flanks in
the mid-1910s. And Norwegian and Swedish immigrants new to
the area formed the Cascade Ski Club in Government Camp in
1928 and staged ski jumping contests on Multorpor Mountain
that drew curious crowds well into the 1930s.

In 1936 the tony Idaho ski resort of Sun Valley had built the
world's first chairlift, which inspired Timberline Lodge to follow
suit with the Magic Mile lift, completed in 1939 and, at the time,
the longest chairlift in the world. Also the first ski lift to use metal
towers, the Magic Mile originally made its way up to about 7,000
feet from much farther east than its current incarnation. Elsewhere
around the mountain, at places like Skibowl and Summit, early
rope tows hauled skiers up for the ride down. Other singularities
from the early days of skiing on Mount Hood: in 1936, a WPA
foreman working on Timberline named Ira Davidson invented
the first-ever snowcat, nicknamed the Snow Kitty, and renowned
Norwegian skier Hjalmar Hvam, who moved to Portland in 1927,
designed and patented the first releasable ski binding after breaking his leg while racing on Mount Hood in 1937—a common

occurrence for skiers in the days prior to breakaway bindings. That same year, the country's first ski patrol, the Mt. Hood Ski Patrol, formed as well.

By the early 1950s, Timberline's troubles notwithstanding, four ski areas on Mount Hood—Timberline, Summit, Skibowl, and Cooper Spur on the north side—were capitalizing on the country's newfound fancy for the schuss. Early in the 1960s several residents of the Hood River Valley had begun scoping out the slopes on Hood's east side for a possible fifth ski area. But in a decision that still tastes bitter to some in the valley, the Forest Service in 1966 awarded the permit for a new ski area instead to Mt. Hood Meadows, an endeavor headed up by Franklin Drake, president of a Portland construction company. The new ski area, now one of the mountain's busiest, opened for business in 1968.

❦

LIKE JEFF KOHNSTAMM over at Timberline Lodge, Matthew Drake basically grew up at a ski resort run by his dad. Born in Portland in 1959, Drake spent the weekends of his childhood at the family cabin in Government Camp, skiing on wooden skis with leather boots and bear-trap bindings in his sister's pink coat. At the close of each weekend, the kids would load up a sled with two days' garbage and race down the road.

"God help you if you wiped out on the garbage sled," said Drake, who later headed east for thirteen years to study economics at Vassar College in New York and work on Wall Street.

Pressed and professional in the company's northwest Portland office, Drake has been CEO at Meadows since his father retired in 2006, though he's almost always been involved with the business. He started his very first job at his father's ski resort the snowy day it opened in 1968. Then eight years old, Drake would stand by a window in The Schuss, Meadows' fast-food grill, and look for arriving guests. When a car would roll in, he'd announce its arrival, grab coffee, hot chocolate, and fresh donuts, and run out in greeting.

"Back then it was just so amazing to have a guest," he said. "The early goings, just like with any startup, were tough. There was a lot of time spent at an activity for which there was a huge amount of passion, but if you looked at the economics of it, it didn't really make a lot of sense."

After a few years of uncertainty, however, and once Highway 35 was kept open year-round, Meadows stabilized and started to do OK. The now 2,150-acre ski area became known for its varied terrain and drier, more powdery snow over on the east side of the mountain. As of 2010 Mt. Hood Meadows averaged 430,000 skiers and snowboarders annually, about 130,000 more than Timberline and in the same ballpark as the resort closest to Portland, Skibowl.

※

IT WAS AT SKIBOWL one day in the early 1980s that Mike Estes saw something that would eventually change his life forever.

A skateboarding punk who spent his high school days bombing down the hills of Government Camp and tearing up the slopes at Skibowl, Estes was a student at Sandy Union High School the day he noticed someone cutting his way down the Lower Bowl at Skibowl. But the guy, one of the lift operators, wasn't on skis. He was on a snowboard.

"I remember when he got to the bottom, the mountain managers came down on him like the Sith lords that they were," Estes said, referencing the evil forces from the Star Wars movies. "The guy lost his job."

Some of the earliest snowboards had been around since the 1960s. Tom Sims, future president of Sims Snowboards, made his first one in shop class in 1963, and Michigan chemical engineer Sherman Poppen introduced the Snurfer in 1965. Even so, and despite the fact that the sport was already flourishing in Vermont by the 1980s, snowboarding was still a relative novelty on Mount Hood when Estes was in high school. In those days, not only did many of the ski areas have strict policies against jumping, but most wanted nothing to do with any newfangled snowboard thingamajig, especially one that didn't have releasable bindings and that could be a huge liability.

On his way out of the ski area, the kid who got fired from Skibowl muttered, in so many words, *Forget this. I'm going to Timberline.*

"A lot of people said the whole snowboarding thing was just a trend," said Jon Tullis, the PR director at Timberline. "But back in its early days, R. L. Kohnstamm said, 'There's good energy here. We need to embrace this.'"

Estes took to snowboarding early on as well, though not without some resistance from his own overlords. A member of his high school ski team—the same one that had produced Bill Johnson, who in 1984 became the first American man to take the Olympic gold medal in downhill skiing—Estes slid into a slump his senior year in 1986. After one particularly frustrating wipeout on the mountain, he stormed back to the team's bus and chucked all his gear. Then, with his coach's eyes bulging out of his head,

Estes grabbed a snowboard a friend had brought onto the bus, strapped his tennis shoes into it, and sailed down the back parking lot.

"I was in huge trouble and got detention," Estes recalled, "but a great thing happened to me right then: I decided I could snowboard."

It wasn't long before Estes and some other trailblazers like Craig Kelly, Dave Dowd, George Pappas, Kris Jamieson, and Mark Hibdon were cutting their way down the slopes at Timberline on early snowboards from Burton, Winterstick, Barfoot, and Sims. And not long after that, with the industry watching Mount Hood, Estes kicked off a fourteen-year stint as a professional snowboarder. He toured the world and eventually had five signature snowboard models from sponsors like Barfoot. A rare battered and bruised Mike Estes Team Freestyle 166 board was up on eBay in 2010 for about $250.

Now forty-three and a sales rep for a few skateboard, bike, and apparel companies, Estes also had a hand in one of Hood's other key snowboarding links: summer camps. Along with John Hartung, owner of the Portland skateboard company Rebel Skates, Estes in 1987 founded the mountain's first summer snowboarding camp, Rebel Boarding School. Though it's no longer around, two other camps have been taking young snowboarders up to Hood's summertime snow for more than twenty years: High Cascade Snowboard Camp based in Government Camp and Windells Camp near Brightwood.

TIM WINDELL is himself a former world champion snowboarder. Inspired by Rob Morrow, a professional boarder in the 1980s who started Morrow Snowboards in Salem, Oregon, Windell cut his teeth on snowboards he made himself in a community college wood shop. By 1988 he was competing on the World Cup Tour of Snowboarding, and by the time he officially retired from the competition circuit in 1991—"When I couldn't keep up with what all those young guys were doing," he said—he'd racked up eight national titles.

Along the way Windell had been running programs for young snowboarders, first up in Whistler, British Columbia, and then on Mount Hood. Since 1991 his namesake camp has called the old Shamrock Hotel on Highway 26 near Sandy its home base; Windell bought the property in 1998. Tucked under tall fir trees just off the road, the plywood and concrete ramps, mountain bike trails, and outbuildings painted with Dr. Seuss characters make the camp look every bit the snowboarding, skateboarding, and skiing retreat that it is. The morning I headed out there, Windell, decked out in a black hoodie, baseball cap, and stubbly shadow, told me about his camp and how important Hood has been to snowboarding.

"In a nutshell, Hood set the pace," he said. "Certainly it's been trumped at times, but it all starts at Hood."

Not only does Hood have the summer snow and the history of Timberline's early snowboarding embrace, but in the late eighties and early nineties, groomers on the mountain like Jeff Flood were experimenting and innovating with ways to sculpt snowboard-friendly terrain. Today, groomers on Hood—including world record holder Rainer Hertrich, who in September 2010 had been skiing in the United States and South America every single day over the prior seven years in an ongoing effort to log 100 million vertical feet—are renowned for their terrain parks and pipes. Every spring the mountain is host to Cutter's Camp, which draws scores of groomers from around the country to learn how to build and maintain the kind of terrain snowboarders and freeskiers crave. One huge jump built at Timberline in the summer of 2010 gave twenty-one-year-old freeskier Sammy Carlson the lift he needed to land the first switch triple rodeo, a jaw-dropping acrobatic move that sent him flying and flipping 150 feet through the high mountain air.

Windell's camp gets about 1,400 campers every summer—mostly young kids but also a few adults—and close to 5,600 the rest of the year, including mountain bikers and twenty-four students who attend a fully accredited high school academy. Staff has included Mike Jankowski, the current freestyle coach for the US Ski Team, and to date, every US athlete who's brought home an Olympic medal in snowboarding has been through Windells, including Shaun White.

"He started here at age six," Windell said, "and by nine he was doing things that we'd never seen a nine-year-old do."

Unfortunately, the day I met Windell, the last of the snowboarders and skiers had already left for the season and the camp and all its action were quiet. A few workers were cleaning out rooms, others were building a street course with ramps and jumps. I tried to picture what it must have been like just a few days earlier, then asked Windell how it is with all those crazy kids there. He cracked a small, honest smile and said one word.

Awesome.

☙

A LITTLE OVER A YEAR after my first ill-fated outing to Skibowl, I was back on the slopes. It was April, so the season was getting late, but twenty-two inches of fresh snow had piled up over the past week. I was solo, as Amy was pregnant with our second child. I learned last-minute that Skibowl was offering free lift tickets for a donation of canned food to benefit the Portland Police Bureau's Sunshine Division, an annual effort that has garnered more than 60,000 pounds of food since 1988. The weather was stellar, I'd gotten the go-ahead from home base, and it was only going to cost me the rentals. I had to go.

Even though I had some trepidation, I felt better that time around. After our first trip to Skibowl the year before, Amy and I had backed off a notch and spent an afternoon at Cooper Spur Mountain Resort, the quaint and practically deserted little ski resort on the north side of the mountain that boasts just one double chairlift for a handful of runs suited to beginners. In the interest of maximizing my opportunity to learn, I'd hopped on the lift, headed up to the top of the 350-foot slope and skied my way down, over and over and over, all afternoon. Amy did not appreciate my pace, but that's the way it went, and it helped.

There at Skibowl again, I felt pretty good. Not overly confident, but assured. I grabbed the tow rope for a few small practice runs, and then headed up the same lift and down the same run from the year before. And lo and behold, I passed the warming hut and actually skied all the way down, upright. Sweet relief.

I spent the afternoon working on my lame wide turns, took out a snowboarder who was trying to steer clear of me, and otherwise got some sort of ski legs going. And as the clouds rolled in and my legs started to tire, I decided that it was indeed time to stop in at the warming hut.

Inside, it was as warm and inviting as I had envisioned it would be: roaring fire, sanguine faces, a shaggy, black-and-tan cat slinking around the oversized log rafters. Framed black-and-white photos on the wall depicted the early glory days of ski jumping on the Multorpor Jump Hill, and a Pilsner Urquell banner incited skiers to drink a pint because "Peter the Mad Czech" did. Peter, it turns out, is Peter Caucus, an Olympic skier from the Czech Republic who supposedly worked at the resort.

I ordered a Black Butte Porter, talked to a guy who was teaching his four-year-old daughter to ski, and soaked in the good energy there at the warming hut.

Turns out, it was a fantastic place for a beer.

UP THE HILL

One cannot defeat or conquer mountains,
one can only climb them.

—Heinrich Harrer, *The White Spider: The Classic*
Account of the Ascent of the Eiger

COLD. CRYSTAL CLEAR. Beautiful. May moonlight magnified the white mountain against a black sky scattered with stars. The breeze was light and fresh, cool and invigorating in the lungs. I felt alive and strong, tense with the energy of anticipation. Everyone was there on Hood's south side, huddled around the climbing register in Timberline's Wy'east Day Lodge: ten students, two assistant guides, and a climb leader, all of us a party of Ptarmigans, the local mountaineering club that as of 2009 had embarked on indefinite hiatus after more than forty years of Cascade enjoyment.

But this was 1999 and the club was invigorated, as were all of us who were there at 6,000 feet about to set out up the South Side route on our first climb of Mount Hood. For the past month or so as part of the Ptarmigans' basic mountaineering course, we'd been poring over The Mountaineers' climbing catchall, *Mountaineering: The Freedom of the Hills,* and gathering in a high school auditorium for weekly sessions on gear and fitness, hydration and altitude, and what to do if we're caught in an avalanche. (Basically swim for your life and hope like hell there's an air pocket in front of your face when the whole mess slams to a halt.)

Weekends had been spent on progressively more difficult hikes: Saddle Mountain in the Coast Range and then to the Columbia River Gorge for Hamilton Mountain, Dog Mountain, and finally, the twelve-mile circuit of a beast whose name alone adds thirty pounds to your pack, Mount Defiance. Contrary to what might seem an obvious inference, this meanest of mountains in the Gorge got its name not from its burly 4,800 feet of elevation, but rather for defying the springtime elements and holding its snow later into the season than any other hill alongside the river.

We'd knocked off Defiance a couple weeks earlier and been greeted at the summit with sunny blue skies and a view of Hood so massive I felt like I could reach out and lay my hands on the mountain's north face.

There on the south side of Mount Hood at 11:15 p.m., spirits were high, the chatter lighthearted and excited. Everyone had a climber's swagger on after signing in. First-timer's swagger, of course, but no matter. If it's your first peak or fiftieth, something about climbing a mountain stiffens the spine, makes it feel OK to be a little headstrong for a change, even if the mountain ultimately ends up having its way with you. Could be the metallic clang of ice ax and crampons on your pack, the burly task ahead and the feat you'll hopefully leave behind, or the very idea that you're climbing a mountain and those folks who just sauntered by on their way into the lodge are not. I know I was feeling it that night—still do at times—and I know everyone in that cold and concrete space had a taste of it as well, even if we were all nervous about whether we'd brought enough water, remembered a map and compass, or if we were in the shape we should have been in.

Climbing Mount Hood was something I'd wanted to do practically since my eyes first took in its sharp white summit two years earlier. Even though I grew up in the flatlands of north-central Ohio in a county whose highest point is a 1,300-foot drive-up hill called Mount Jeez—as in, *Jeez, isn't the view from up here amazing?* (and it is, especially in autumn or during summertime meteor showers)—I felt naturally pulled toward the mountain and its top. I wasn't a climber. I had only recently started backpacking and seriously hiking, and knew little about what it would take to climb a Cascade mountain, or even if you could.

And then, one dark and late spring night around a wild campfire at Oswald West State Park on the Oregon Coast, someone told me you could walk to the top of Mount Hood in sneakers.

That's it, I thought right then. *To the top of the mountain.*

JOEL PALMER didn't ever walk to the very top of Mount Hood, nor did he own a pair of sneakers. But in 1845 the Canadian-born pioneer became the first known white man to ascend and explore Hood's very upper reaches. The renowned Scottish botanist David Douglas may have headed high up on the mountain himself in 1833, but a near-fatal drop over a waterfall on British

Columbia's Fraser River that same year swallowed up his journal and washed away any definitive proof for later generations.

Palmer's log, however, originally published in 1847 as *Journal of Travels: On the Oregon Trail in 1845*, survives. Over just four of its 300-plus pages, Palmer nonchalantly details the push he made toward the top of the mountain on October 12, 1845, essentially alone and in moccasins that eventually blew out and left him in bare feet somewhere above 9,500 feet on Hood's south side, a push that unknowingly kicked off a long and colorful story of Mount Hood climbing.

Born October 4, 1810, in Elizabethtown, Ontario, Palmer grew up in a Quaker family who hurried to New York's Catskill Mountains at the outbreak of the War of 1812. After four years of indentured servitude with another Quaker family, a sixteen-year-old Palmer struck out to explore the world a bit. He landed first in Philadelphia and then headed to Laurel, Indiana, where he worked as a canal-building contractor before being elected to his first of two terms in the state legislature in 1843.

But Palmer was a moving man, and in his *Journal of Travels* he notes that the "great inducements" of the Oregon Territory proved too tantalizing to keep him in Indiana. So in 1845, Palmer temporarily left his family behind and headed west on the Oregon Trail. With various parties, he traveled across Missouri, Nebraska, Wyoming, Idaho, and on into Oregon, where he ran smack dab into a Columbia River bottleneck at The Dalles, a riverside settlement at the end of the Oregon Trail. Seems Palmer wasn't the only pioneer in search of Oregon's inducements, and with only two boats ferrying travelers and their wagons downstream—for a sum worth more than the cargo alone—no one was going anywhere very fast. Throw in a food and livestock feed shortage, and it's no wonder Palmer got antsy and opted to head south, in search of an overland route through a mountain pass to Oregon City, the first incorporated city west of the Rocky Mountains.

Along with fifteen other families in a train of twenty-three wagons, Palmer set off and in just a few days came upon the wagons of Samuel K. Barlow near the White River on the southeast side of Mount Hood. Convicted but pardoned of manslaughter—he'd killed a man with an ax in Indiana—Barlow had made his own way west with his family, then stormed out of the backup at The Dalles, declaring that God had never made a mountain without some way to get around it.

The two men combined their teams and continued their journey together, clearing thick growths of wild rhododendrons, tall firs, and cedars with axes, saws, and the pioneer equivalent of prescribed burning. But the going was slow—slower than the approach of winter—and if the train didn't find the pass soon, it was either back to The Dalles or, quite likely, on to the great beyond.

Faced with such a grim prospect, Palmer, Barlow, and a man identified in Palmer's writings only as Mr. Lock, set off in front of the train in search of the pass. They powered their way up through the forest and along the White River to the wide, pumice-strewn plains that afford a truly stunning view of the mountain.

"I had never before looked upon a sight so nobly grand," Palmer wrote in his journal on October 11, 1845. "No pen can give an adequate description of this scene."

Palmer and his cohorts moved on and soon found themselves switchbacking their way down a yawning canyon, crossing a rapid stream at the bottom, and then zigzagging back up the other side. His journal directions for this crossing—". . . go zigzag for about one hundred yards, then turn short round, and go zigzag until you come under the place where you started from . . ."—are why Mount Hood today has a Zigzag Canyon, a Zigzag River, a Zigzag Glacier, and the village of Zigzag.

The next morning the threesome headed up the mountain from their campsite in what is presumed to have been near today's Paradise Park in search of a better vantage point. Palmer was gung ho and cracked the whip to goad Barlow and Lock up over the massive cliff at the head of Zigzag Canyon, now known as Mississippi Head. The latter two bellyached and instead sat down, saying Palmer should go on and signal if he found an easy way up. So he did, climbing a forty-foot cliff of snow and ice by chopping holds for his hands and feet. With his moccasins worn out and his bare feet now exposed to the snow, Palmer climbed on, knocking off the rest of the cliff and continuing up the mountain for at least another mile before having a seat atop a pile of rocks.

"I then rolled stones down the mountain for half an hour," Palmer wrote, "but as I could see nothing of my two friends, I began to suspect that they had gone back."

Based upon his description, Palmer was likely very near Illumination Rock. He then continued east and up a little farther, possibly approaching Crater Rock at 10,000 feet, surveyed the land below in search of a passable route for the wagon train—a route that would later become the Barlow Road, the main passage through the Cascades for countless Oregon Trail pioneers—and began his descent. Likely hoofing it down the small glacier named after him in 1924, Palmer describes a treacherous undertaking down an ice sheet full of "deep ravines and crevices" and "hideous looking caverns."

Once reunited with Barlow, Lock, and ultimately the entire party on the White River, Palmer dispelled as erroneous the popular assertion that Mount Hood could not be climbed to its summit. On the contrary, he said: not only could Mount Hood be climbed, but so could any other of the snowy peaks in the range. Palmer then even suggested the best route for topping out on Hood.

"I think the southern side affords the easiest ascent," he wrote, not knowing at all that one day, Hood would become one of the most-climbed mountains in the world with thousands of prospective summiteers trudging up its snowy flanks, primarily those of its south side, every year.

THAT WAS US, boots—not moccasins or sneakers—crunching through the snow just above Timberline Lodge on our way up the eastern edge of Palmer's namesake snowfield. Though Hood's summit has likely been trodden by a pair of Nikes, stiff plastic boots or leather ones with steel shanks are standard footwear, not only for keeping out the cold and wet snow, but for affixing crampons to for the steep upper slopes.

The early stretch is relatively flat, so there was still plenty of banter between us, even if we had to try a little harder to be heard above the gathering winds. Our first milestone, Silcox Hut, was visible just above at about 7,000 feet. We reached it for our first official break about an hour into the climb. At the time, Silcox was open to passing climbers, who could stop in for some food, drink, and a brief warm-up by the roaring hearth.

All of which made it hard to peel ourselves away from Silcox and head back out into the chilly night. But as nice as Silcox was, and despite rumors of a fresh keg of beer on the way, it was not our goal. The summit was, so we headed back out.

❦

NO ONE KNOWS for sure whether or not any Native Americans stood on the mountain's summit before the first whites did, but it's not very likely. Most of the tribes known to live in the area— among them the Kalapuya, upper Chinooks, Molallas, and Warm Springs—revered and feared the mountain and so stayed away from its upper regions. Some believed that only death awaited those who climbed.

Not so the white man.

After Palmer came a party who actually set out to climb Mount Hood not for botanical or navigational reasons, but simply to be the first. The group included William Barlow, son of Samuel; William O. Travaillot, a retired sea merchant who in 1851 had become one of Portland's first arrested citizens for riding his horse "at a furious rate through the streets"; Granville Haller; Cyrus Olney; Wells Lake; and an unidentified Native American guide. Leading the party was Thomas Jefferson Dryer, a gruff newspaperman with a penchant for stiff drinks, editorial repartee, and alpine quests. He founded the *Weekly Oregonian*— today's *Oregonian*—in 1850 and bagged the first recorded summit of Mount St. Helens on August 26, 1853. He also once challenged a Portland merchant to a duel with rifles over an outstanding advertising debt.

After convening in a canyon below timberline, Dryer and his team likely headed up a ridge separating the White River and the East Fork Hood River on the morning of August 8, 1854. Haller bailed after becoming dizzy, Olney once the slopes became too steep, and Travaillot after finding what Dryer described as "blood starting from the surface." The others climbed on until they reached what Dryer would call the summit sometime around midafternoon. In a write-up of the climb in an 1854 issue of *Littell's Living Age*, Dryer described the mountain's topmost ridge and its volcanic debris, including cones twenty to fifty feet tall and vents spewing hot, sulfurous gasses. The view, Dryer wrote, included St. Helens, Adams, Rainier, Jefferson, and Mount Shasta, 275 miles away in California.

But Dryer's description made no note of two prominent lakes, today's Lost Lake and Bull Run Lake, or the mighty Columbia River, all plainly visible in clear weather to the north from the summit. People may not have known it at the time, but the intervening mountains and the curvature of the earth make it physically impossible to see Shasta from Hood. Add in a measurement that Dryer's party made that put Hood's elevation at more than 18,300 feet, and eyebrows back in Portland were bound to raise.

But though some may have questioned the party's estimation of Hood's height, no one really disputed their claim to the summit—until three years later.

On August 6, 1857, one of Dryer's employees, a twenty-two-year-old typesetter named Henry J. Pittock, joined a party of four other men who staked their horses at timberline, filled their pockets with provisions, and headed for the true summit of

Hood. The others in the party included W. Lyman Chittenden, L. J. Powell, James Deardorff, and William Buckley.

In a letter to the editor of the *Democratic Standard*, another Portland newspaper, on August 13, 1857, Deardorff recounted the climb in detail, tracing the party's steps up snowfields and ridges, past volcanic rocks, down into a cave for a little side trip, over a crevasse, and on up to the summit, where they gave "nine hearty cheers" and carved their names in the rock. Although Deardorff likely misidentified Mount Adams as Mount Olympus and a southern Cascade peak as Mount Shasta, his description of the summit was otherwise much more accurate and realistic than Dryer's. In his letter, Deardorff suggests that the Dryer party must have topped out about 350 feet below the true summit on the exposed ridge known today as the Steel Cliff. There are no volcanic vents up top, Deardorff noted, and unlike the top of the Steel Cliff down below, the actual summit isn't nearly as expansive as Dryer had reported.

Dryer was livid.

In a *Weekly Oregonian* editorial two days later, Dryer called Deardorff and his fellow climbers "panting aspirants" who were merely "anxious for fame, distinction and notoriety." He also rebuked the youngsters for disrespecting their elders.

"Well, these young gentlemen may learn . . . that to become great or good men, they must learn the elementary principles that constitute gentlemen; they must not measure the veracity of those far their seniors in years, experience and standing, with their panting desire for fame. A little modesty and prudence sometimes saves young men a good deal of trouble . . ."

Yet nowhere in his written tongue-lashing did Dryer try to explain the discrepancies or refute Deardorff's assertions. A man of great personal pride, Dryer may not have been able to admit that perhaps he'd not been the first to stand on Hood's true summit after all. And so the credit for the actual first summit of Mount Hood belongs to Pittock and his cohorts.

In an odd twist of fate a few years later, Pittock would end up taking ownership of the *Weekly Oregonian* from Dryer in 1860 as payment for back salary.

As for Dryer, who ultimately landed a federal commissioner appointment in Hawaii, topping out on the Steel Cliff at almost 11,000 feet—in 1854 no less—was no small feat in its own right. Later detractors, including William G. Steel, the cliff's namesake and founder of Crater Lake National Park and the Mazamas mountaineering club, continued to balk, saying there was no way Dryer could have taken the route he said he had. Physically impossible, they scoffed. But in 1890, a young mountaineer named William Langille, known for pioneering climbs on Hood's north face and the name behind one of the mountain's eleven glaciers, actually traveled the upper sections of Dryer's route and blazed his way to the top for a champagne toast. The climb, called the Wy'east route, is still popular today.

TRUDGING UP from Silcox, the moon still lit our way, and off in the darkness to the south rose a grand, gray shadow—Mount Jefferson. The terrain here was white and gradual and quiet for a stretch, but then it started to angle upward noticeably. The pace of our group slowed in direct proportion to the slope. At the top of the Palmer chairlift and the road that the snowcats flattened out, we unbuckled for another break. As we were sipping drinks and downing energy bars, a blue-eyed redhead named Tracy stopped short.

I don't feel so good, she said, then promptly folded herself forward into the snow. Al, our lead guide, steadied her, but as she tried to stand, down she went. Out cold.

No one said a word as Al searched for signs in her pupils.

Then just like that, Tracy opened her eyes and was back with us. Kind of. She was very aware, but obviously wouldn't be going any higher. That's not a risk that anyone— climber, guide, whoever—would ever be willing to take. We bid her and a few supporters farewell and headed up as they headed down.

I never found out what happened to Tracy or how the return trip down the mountain was, but later, after the climb was over and we were rolling down Highway 26 back to Portland, talk turned to Silent Rock. You pass through it on the way up to Mount Hood from Portland at mile forty-nine, just a few miles west of Government Camp. There, the road makes a long bend south between two high rock faces that were once part of the same massive outcropping. Engineers rerouting the highway needed the road to go through that rock, not around it, so they blasted a passage.

Depending on who you talk to up on the mountain, the dynamite may have either disturbed a sacred burial ground or unleashed a rock slide that killed a young Native American boy walking through the trees down below. In a gesture of respect to whatever souls may have been disturbed there, and to ensure a safe trip to the mountain, you're supposed to be silent while passing through.

Whether or not the legend is true—a friend, Dennis Kraft, who has a cabin in Government Camp, posited that an irritated school bus driver may have concocted the tale of the little boy as a way to temporarily zip the lips of his passengers on their way up to the mountain—I've abided by it ever since learning about it on that first climb.

Why?

Because I remember hearing soon after that first climb of Hood that although everyone in our car had been mum through Silent Rock on the way up to Mount Hood, one person in the car ahead of us had not.

Tracy.

AFTER PITTOCK'S PARTY summited the mountain, climbing on Mount Hood slowly began to pick up. Various groups trudged up the South Side route over the ensuing years, including the first women to summit in 1867. Most climbers usually traveled by horseback either to Government Camp or camps at timberline. Their implements were crude—hand-cut staves for hiking sticks, charcoal from their campfires for sun block—but they climbed and they summited.

They also pioneered new paths to the top. By 1892 climbers had made first ascents of Cathedral Ridge on the northwest face, Wy'east on the east side, and the Cooper Spur and Sunshine routes on Hood's northern reaches. Hood climbing legend Elijah Coalman spearheaded the effort to build a fire lookout cabin on the summit of the mountain in 1915, and from its construction until its abandonment in 1933, rangers manning the cabin would annually install fixed lines on the upper portions of the Cooper Spur and South Side routes to accommodate climbers. A ladder spanning the bergschrund on the south side also helped climbers reach the top.

By 1939 most of the other major routes on the mountain had been blazed, including Castle Crags, high on the western edge of the crater, and the Leuthold Couloir, named for Joseph Leuthold, one of the founders of the Mt. Hood Ski Patrol. Leuthold, along with Russ McJury, also nabbed the first ascents of the Sandy Headwall and Eliot Headwall routes. One of the final routes to fall on Hood was Yocum Ridge, smack in the middle of the mountain's western profile. Named for Oliver Yocum, an early climbing guide and hotelier in Government Camp, the ridge is a toothy, exposed, steep mess of rotten rock with no inclination for protection or holds. Storied Northwest climber Fred Beckey and his climbing partner Leo Scheiblehner finally knocked it off in early April 1959, climbing up its fragile, feathered ice that at times was supported underneath by little more than daylight. Beckey later described the route as "a nightmare of ice problems instead of a route to the summit."

DESPITE A COUPLE successful variations of Yocum Ridge and a few other routes, not much ground was left to be broken on Mount Hood after Beckey and Scheiblehner's ascent of Yocum. But during a solo ski traverse around the mountain in 1987, an ambitious climber became intrigued.

Raised in Portland from age three, Wayne Wallace grew up with Hood. His parents would take him hiking up on the mountain as a kid, and he learned to ski its slopes early on. As a teenager he got a job at the Huckleberry Inn in Government Camp—a

longtime local favorite spot for huckleberry pancakes and pies—
and at sixteen, he and a friend had an epic trip on the Timberline
Trail that left them both laid up in the hospital. He first climbed
Hood in 1982—"That was my awakening in terms of climbing,"
he said—honeymooned with his first wife up there, and spent a
first date with his current girlfriend of fourteen years climbing at
Illumination Rock.

"I have so many connections with the mountain," he said.

While on that solo ski traverse in 1987, Wallace was round-
ing the eastern edge of the peak just around the corner from
Cooper Spur when he saw a nearly untouched wall high up on
its face at about 10,000 feet. The wall and its potential had earlier come to Wallace's attention after he'd read some published
inquiries about it from Jeff Thomas, author of the classic *Oregon
High: A Climbing Guide to Nine Cascade Volcanoes*. Full of rotten rock but boasting fantastic lines of seasonal ice and snow to
the summit, the face elicits images of the Eiger in Switzerland.
It's known as the Black Spider, and was possibly first climbed by
storied Oregon climber Ted Davis.

Wallace, known as an intense, accomplished, and sometimes unorthodox climber—he once climbed the tough Eliot
Headwall after an all-night party, according to longtime climbing
partner Tim Olson—became obsessed.

"Wayne's traditional method of climbing and his intensity
is not like everybody else's," said Olson, who himself pioneered an
obscure route at Hood's western base in 1991. Called the Gilette
Arette, the route is on the Razorblade Pinnacle, possibly a remnant of the Sandy Glacier volcano that predates Hood.

Wallace set about tackling routes on the Black Spider. In
February of 1994 he and his climbing partner Steve Elder made

the first ascent of the main wall. Twenty-three years after he first saw the Black Spider, Wallace put to rest one of his longest-running obsessions when he and partner Beau Carrillo finally hit the summit up a line on the face Wallace calls Center Drip.

The fact that there are still several unclimbed routes on the Black Spider and also over on Illumination Rock leads both Wallace and Olson to believe that there's still more to be done on Mount Hood.

"You keep looking up there at that mountain," Olson said, "and thinking—I wonder?"

HIGHER UP ON THE Palmer Snowfield, the slope steepened and iced up enough for crampons. White and yellow lights from other climbers swayed in the darkness below like fireflies. Off in the east, the first shades of sunrise had begun to lighten the lower horizon, and by the time we'd made it up to Crater Rock at 10,000 feet, Hood's pyramidal shadow spread out across the valley floor. It's a glorious image, backed by the soft colors and fresh air of dawn, and also an exclusive one reserved almost entirely for those who stand high on the mountain's shoulders on clear and early mornings. Seeing the world from somewhere new, somewhere different, and taking in such singular views is by far one of the great joys of climbing a mountain, any mountain.

Onward and upward, we crested the Hogsback, a long and graceful ridge of snow deposited by wind along the Coalman Glacier that channels climbers in a near single-file lane toward the summit. Here we lost another climber—spent and tired, she'd started seeing white flashes in her eyes—and broke up into a couple different rope teams. Many climbers rope up on the Hogsback, the thought being that if one climber takes a tumble on the steeper upper slopes of Hood, the others tied into the rope will be able to help arrest the fall. This approach, assuming it works when it needs to, would be most helpful above the bergschrund, the gaping crevasse that cleaves the Hogsback about halfway across its length. In another school of thought, many climbers choose not to rope up on the South Side at all because if that one climber takes a tumble and those others on the rope aren't able to arrest the fall—a likely scenario if conditions are icy and no anchors have been placed—then you've got a whole tangle of bodies careening down the mountain.

Tied together now, we inched our way up the Hogsback in the early sunlight and took an unnerving step over a receding snow bridge barely spanning the bergschrund. Deep down in the crack the ice looked blue and bottomless. Above and all around the mountain's upper amphitheater, beautiful rime ice formations clung to the crater walls like billowing white smoke. From inside the jacket of one climber we passed peered a dachshund with big Oakley sunglasses taped to its face; a little higher, two snowboarders smoked cigarettes during a break on their way up.

The final few hundred feet stair-stepped up through the Pearly Gates, a narrow and steep chute filigreed with snow and ice. In 2006 winds shifted the snow of the Hogsback to the west just enough to make the climb up through the Pearly Gates much steeper, more technical, and, therefore, much less accessible than it used to be. The standard route these days instead heads up a face west of the Hogsback known as the Old Chute and ends with a traverse along a narrow and exposed ridge to the summit. One stretch of this ridge requires a good thirty feet of nothing but steely focus on every single step. Slipping to the right along this traverse to the summit would send you crashing down a long, steep slope; slip the other way, down into the scenic void just a foot or so off your left boot, and you may not hit much for a thousand feet or so. Best not to gaze too long into that abyss.

OVER THE YEARS the mountain has been host to a range of unique climbing feats and stories not readily found on other Cascadian peaks. In 1894, in response to an advertisement in the newspaper, more than one hundred people climbed to the top of Mount Hood and formed the Mazamas outdoor club. Still requisite for membership in the club, which took its name from the Spanish word for mountain goat, is topping out on a glaciated peak. Illumination Rock, the signature outcropping on Hood's southwest corner, got its name in the late nineteenth century, when several climbing parties lit up the mountain for Portlanders with pounds of something called red fire, probably a powder of strontium salts similar to what's used in modern flares. In 1915 a local couple tied the knot on the top; the reception followed in the summit tent of Elijah Coalman, who served up breakfast for the party of nearly twenty. In 1931 three members of the Cascade Ski Club, including well-known sportsman Hjalmar Hvam, made the first ski ascent and descent of the mountain. Nine climbers carried a disassembled bicycle to the summit in August of 1947, put it back together, and took turns pedaling around. A tree-dwelling ape known as a gibbon—and named Kandy—reached the summit on the back of a Portland pet store owner in 1964, and in 1973 six blind teenagers climbed to the top. The youngest people to ever make the summit were five-year-old Harry Callicotte in 1936 and Penelope White, also five, in 1974.

More than a few dogs have also found their way up Mount Hood. The most famous, a mixed-breed collie from Government Camp named Ranger, joined random climbing parties throughout the early 1930s and sometimes summited twice in the same day. By the time he'd climbed on to the great mountain in the sky in 1940, Ranger was believed to have made the top nearly 500 times. Suitably, he was buried on the summit. And Caddis, a yellow lab, holds the official timed speed record for an ascent of the mountain by man and man's best friend: she and her climbing partner, Portlander Dan Howitt, climbed to the summit from Timberline Lodge in one hour and fifty-seven minutes in 2004.

HALFWAY UP through the Pearly Gates, the excruciatingly slow pace of Hood's South Side climb on a beautiful spring day allowed us some time to make small talk with a few teams picking their way down through the softening snow. Just smiles and hellos at first, but then something more. Two climbers. Fell. Cooper Spur. The north face.

It was all just trickling rumors right then and there. But I know in that moment I was focused on the summit—could see it just 500 feet higher—and to hear something like that just then did not fit into my perception of what it was going to be like to stand on top of Mount Hood for the very first time. I distinctly remember word coming down through the ranks that someone had possibly fallen near the summit, but for better or worse in that moment, it didn't stick with me or jolt me the way it probably should have.

And then finally, a full nine hours after we'd set out from Timberline Lodge, the summit of Mount Hood. We'd made it, and it was worth it. Unbelievable views of the Cascades, from Rainier, Adams, and St. Helens in the north to Jefferson, the Three Sisters, and beyond in the south. The Columbia River. The Oregon desert out east. Lakes and clear-cuts like panels on an evergreen quilt down below. The Willamette Valley and the lowlands of Portland to the west. Above, a cerulean sky so deep in hue as to appear convex.

Hood's proper summit is a broad, snowy slope that someone once described as about the size of a tennis court. There's plenty of room for summit photos and respite—and scores of other climbers. During a weekend spring climb, it is no place for solitude. But no one who's even remotely familiar with climbing on Hood expects anything different. The mountain is close to the Portland metro region and its two million people; its South Side is, as Palmer predicted, an accessible way to the top, and if you're in decent shape and get at least a tad bit lucky, you have a good shot at actually making the summit. It's also an amazingly beautiful peak to climb and stand atop. All of which makes Mount Hood a nearly irresistible mountain for alpinists of all persuasions. Mount St. Helens and Mount Adams both offer similar climbing appeal relatively nearby and attract their own hordes, but Hood's South Side is by far king when it comes to crowds.

In 1999 the Forest Service toyed with the idea of a permit system to limit the number of climbers on the South Side route during peak season weekends. At the time, about 215 climbers clogged the route each weekend day during the prime climbing window; the Forest Service's plan would have cut that number to just twenty-five. Not surprisingly, the idea didn't sit too well with many people, and so the Forest Service tucked it away for another day.

It's an idea that's almost surely going to come back around, however, as the Portland population continues to swell, the demands put upon the mountain increase, and an accident made worse by too many climbers on the South Side route morphs from potential to reality. On another climb up, more than ten years after my first summit that incredibly included a near full moon and a lunar eclipse, I sat on the Hogsback in midmorning and counted no fewer than sixty-two people in the main chute to the summit ridge. Even more alarming, many of them looked barely prepared enough for a trip to the grocery store, let alone to the top of an 11,000-foot glaciated mountain. One team of at least eight people, tied together by a climbing rope around their waists without any harnesses, carried just a pack or two between them, another climber said he'd seen a team sharing crampons, the members wearing just one on each foot.

UNLESS YOU ARE A skier or snowboarder who's carried your gear up with you for what appears to be a great ride down, descending the south side of Mount Hood from its summit is quite a drag. Because we'd arrived on top so late in the morning—nine o'clock on a warm Sunday in May, with a bright sun softening the snow into a dangerous slush that tends to clog up in crampons—we spent just fifteen minutes on the summit before turning around and heading down. The same bottleneck in the Pearly Gates from the

way up awaited our descent, but even after that delay, the slog down
was little more than one step in front of the other. Occasionally,
harder patches of snow afforded a decent *glissade*—essentially sled-
ding down on a pair of rain pants, a plastic bag, a shovel, or anything else you might have with you—but overall it was little more
than a trudge. Timberline Lodge, visible from the summit all the
way back down, teased like a mirage in the distance and never
seemed to get one step closer. Those lucky enough to have snowboards or skis seemed to be mocking us as they sailed off in glee.
The cruelest vision: the ski lift lightly ferrying riders up to 8,500
feet and all those empty chairs gliding back down all alone. What
I would have given for a ride down that last 2,500 feet.

But no. When you climb Mount Hood's South Side from
Timberline Lodge on your own two feet, that's exactly how you
come down, assuming all goes well. And in a way, that made the
first step on pavement that much more gratifying once we'd finally
made it back to the parking lot four hours after gazing across the
state from its highest point. Beat but energized, accomplished yet
spent, we cracked celebration beers, toasted the mountain from
the relative safety of the parking lot, and then piled in for the ride
back home. We had been to the top of the mountain, and surely
it was grand.

ACCIDENT

*Your friends may die up there in the clouds, in storms,
swept away by avalanches, or cowering under a volley
of stones. Perhaps they'll freeze to death alone at the
bottom of a deep, dark crevasse or sit down to rest and
never get up again. This is the long fall, where the sky is
rose and the mountains have never been as beautiful as
they are today.*

—MARK TWIGHT, "A Lifetime Before Death"

TENA CARDON AND HER HUSBAND, Carey, had climbed
together for years: Hood, the Three Sisters, Rainier—just
about all of the major Cascades. The couple spent their weekends
in the mountains or hanging out at local crags honing their climbing skills. Even when they were at home in Hillsboro, Oregon,
climbing stayed on their minds. They worked out religiously,
pounding away on the StairMasters at their local gym, and even
strapped on their crampons to aerate their lawn.

By 1998 the Cardons had set a goal to climb the continent's
highest peak—Alaska's 20,320-foot Denali—in 2000. Training

toward that milestone found them on the slopes of Mount Hood in the spring of 1999. The weekend of May 15, sketchy avalanche conditions had turned Tena, 29, and Carey, 31, back from a summit attempt via the Cooper Spur route on Hood's northeast face. Named for David Rose Cooper, a Scotsman who settled in the Hood River Valley in 1882 and became one of the first climbing guides on the mountain, Cooper Spur was once the most popular route up Mount Hood. A classic photo from the Mazamas shows a string of early alpinists, including several women in floor-length dresses, ascending Cooper Spur during the club's inaugural climb in 1894.

Over the years, however, Cooper Spur has gained a notorious reputation as one of the most dangerous routes on the mountain. Its upper reaches are steep—some say fifty degrees or more—and a fall from here often sends climbers plummeting nearly 2,000 feet to the Eliot Glacier below. During a descent from the summit in 1961, Colin Chisholm and his son, Douglas, took such a spill, plunging 2,000 feet over the headwall in an avalanche, landing on the glacier, and miraculously surviving with only minor injuries. Since then, that fall off Cooper Spur has been known as the Chisholm Trail. To date, at least fifteen people who've taken the trail have not been as lucky as the Chisholms.

THE WEEKEND AFTER they'd turned around, the Cardons headed back to the mountain and pitched an orange tent at about 7,000 feet, just up from Cloud Cap Inn and on the way up Cooper Spur. At around 4:30 a.m. on Sunday, May 23, the two set out for the summit. The morning was a beautiful one of crystal-clear skies and gentle alpine breezes, just as it had been for us over on the South Side the very same morning. The early sunrise colored the horizon and brightened the snowy slope of Cooper Spur. It also softened the snow early. According to the May 24, 1999, edition of the *Oregonian*, the freezing level the Friday morning of that weekend had been at 8,000 feet; by that Sunday morning, when the Cardons were on their way up, it had risen to 13,400 feet. By the time they were just 300 feet from the summit, the slushy snow was already balling up in their crampons.

The couple topped out at 8:00 a.m., about the time we were stepping over the bergschrund down below. They congratulated each other, soaked in the view for five minutes, and prepared to head down. Another team that had come up Cooper Spur just behind Tena and Carey opted to descend the less exposed South Side because of the deteriorating snow conditions on Cooper Spur. They were surprised to learn that the Cardons were heading back down the spur and even considered offering the couple a ride back around to the north side to recover their tent if they wanted to hoof it down the relative safety of the South Side.

Instead, Tena and Carey Cardon, still roped together, left the summit of Mount Hood that morning on the same route they'd come up. Within ten minutes of their departure, climbers relaxing and celebrating on the summit heard someone scream.

ALSO ON HIS WAY UP the mountain's south side that May weekend was Steve Boyer, a Portland emergency room physician with more than his share of experience in the mountains. Soft-spoken and trim after decades of climbing, biking, and running—he grew up chasing sheep and cattle on a ranch in Wyoming and ran alongside future Olympic marathoner Frank Shorter on the track team at Yale—Boyer has summited the 26,200-foot south face of Annapurna, been to 28,000 feet on Everest, and climbed the frozen grass of the Shepherd's Pillar on Poland's Giewont massif. He was on the 1986 K2 expedition with Alan Pennington and John Smolich, the two Silcox Hut boosters killed by an avalanche. Boyer's also climbed Hood 160 times, ridden his bike from Portland to Timberline for a climb and then ridden back home—in just over ten hours—and run the entire forty-one-mile Timberline Trail in just under seven hours.

Boyer didn't hear the Cardons' screams, but he arrived at the summit soon after and took in reports of their fall. One climber had already been lowered down about four rope lengths in a vain attempt to try and help the couple or at least see what may have happened. By then, the snow on the upper slopes of the north face had turned to slush, ruling any kind of climbing descent down Cooper Spur almost out of the question. But Boyer had another idea.

"The conditions on Cooper Spur weren't any good for climbing," he said, "but they were OK for skiing."

Pictures of the ski descent of Cooper Spur are enough to elicit sweaty palms and tingling anxiety in mere mortals. The lines look impossibly steep, the airy exposure absolutely frightening. If you didn't know better, you might think you were skiing off the summit into the clear, thin air.

"It's very unnerving because it's convex, so you can't see the bottom," Boyer said.

Nonetheless, he strapped on his skis and angled down, at first testing the snow while on a rope. Once comfortable, he untied and headed down the spur in search of the Cardons.

Down the doctor went, making one crucial turn at a rock band toward the Eliot Headwall and then cutting back over to the spur. He carved his way down the headwall, jumped the bergschrund, and landed squarely on the Eliot Glacier. A little higher up the glacier at about 9,400 feet—2,000 feet below the summit—was Hood climbing ranger Glen Kessler, who'd skied around the mountain from the south side once he'd heard about the accident. Boyer climbed up to Kessler and, nearby, the lifeless and still roped together bodies of Tena and Carey Cardon. Carey had his crampons on; one of Tena's had fallen off and the other looked broken. The immediate supposition was that the slushy snow had balled up in their crampons and caused one of them to slip on the steep slope. Because they were tied together, both slid down the Chisholm Trail and plummeted 1,500 feet to the Eliot Glacier below.

When Boyer arrived at the scene, Tena was sitting upright in the snow with her helmet on. Hunks of snow and ice, disturbed by the warming sun and the climbers' fall, randomly thudded onto the glacier near Boyer. Usually religious about wearing his helmet, especially when skiing the upper 1,500 feet of Mount Hood, Boyer had forgotten his that day.

"So I borrowed her helmet," he said. "It felt kind of weird, but it was what I needed to do."

BEAUTIFUL. EXHILARATING. SUBLIME. Climbing mountains evokes a litany of colorful descriptors, matched only by the span of reasoning behind each individual's inspiration. Everest prospector George Mallory's well-trodden "Because it's there" touched on the quotidian reality of slogging up a mountain, while John Muir's "Climb the mountains and get their good tidings . . ." evoked a loftier sense of spirituality connected with higher vantage points.

But climbing also comes laced with another set of elements—risk and danger, which can, on the one hand, accentuate the power and intensity of a mountain experience; on the other, they, along with poor judgment, gear failure, and pure, cruel chance, can get people killed.

"The mountain's not evil, it's not mean, but if you're in the wrong place at the wrong time, bad things can happen," said Timberline Lodge's Jeff Kohnstamm. The landmark hotel almost always serves as a staging ground for search and rescue crews and family members when something goes awry on Hood.

In more than 150 years of climbing, no fewer than 138 people have lost their lives on Mount Hood. Great falls, terrible weather, avalanches, boulders, blocks of ice, poisonous gas, bad decisions, ill preparedness, or some combination of these have been behind most of them. The first on the mountain—which is also listed as the first recorded recreational mountain climbing fatality in the country—found Portland grocer Frederic Kirn swept off the mountain in a rockslide high on Cooper Spur in July of 1896. His body was found the next day nearly 400 feet below on the Newton Clark Glacier.

The ensuing century or so saw an average of just over one fatality per year. During a 103-person Mazama climb of the Sunshine route up Hood's north side in the summer of 1927, one climber on a rope team of ten slipped on a snowfield, triggering a 600-foot slide that sent the entire team barreling down the slope, over an icy cliff, and onto the lower lip of a gaping crevasse. Despite numerous injuries, the fall resulted in only a single death, that of Portland dentist Stanton Stryker, who'd been run through the chest by a long, sharp climbing staff known as an alpenstock.

A twenty-two-year-old University of Washington student named Victor von Normann died on August 27, 1934, after successfully climbing the mountain via the South Side route. On the way down, he and a friend had been intrigued enough by one of the larger fumaroles near Crater Rock that they climbed down into it. Within minutes, carbon dioxide and poisonous sulfur overwhelmed von Normann, who stumbled and tumbled close to 200 feet to the cavern floor. His friend, Edward Tremper, barely made it back out alive; the same went for several rescuers who tried and finally succeeded in recovering von Normann's body from the depths.

As with the fall down the Chisholm Trail on the north side, Hood's south side has its own classic and tragic line, but one of different consequence. Clopping down from the summit in clear weather, it's easy for climbers to make their way back to Timberline Lodge because they can see it along the entire route. But if clouds, fog, or snow set in, and if someone doesn't know how to use a compass or GPS, the route back to Timberline is less than straightforward. That's because of something known as the *fall line*, which is essentially the natural and gravitational path down the mountain. Drop a ball down the south side of Mount Hood from Crater Rock, and the natural thought is that it will make its way south back to Timberline Lodge. Not so.

The fall line actually pulls southwesterly below Crater Rock, just enough to draw wandering climbers off course, away from the Palmer ski lift and Timberline Lodge and toward the gaping chasm of Zigzag Canyon. Another hazard just above the canyon: Mississippi Head, a sheer, 400-foot buttress benignly named for a delegation of newspaper editors from Mississippi who visited Portland in 1905. The navigational mistake down the fall line has occurred over and over, so much so that the area between the summit, Timberline Lodge, and just west of Zigzag Canyon has been dubbed the Mount Hood Triangle. Those who find themselves coming down the south side in whiteout conditions are able to avoid the perils of the triangle and find their way back to Timberline by setting a compass bearing of magnetic due south and sticking to it, no matter how unnatural it may feel.

One of the triangle's early episodes happened on March 31, 1940, soon after Gerald Herrmann and James Lorentz summited Hood by way of the South Side in swirling snow and frigid temperatures. In the summit register, they scratched out nothing more than "March 31, too cold to write." That weekend, a fierce storm had blown in from the Pacific, ripping the roof off Newport High School on the Oregon Coast, tossing a car over a seaside bluff, and knocking down telephone poles across Portland. Though it's a wonder why the two climbers were up on the mountain with such volatile weather swarming about in the first place, it's no surprise that they had trouble descending through the dreadful wind and snow.

Once they got below Crater Rock at 10,000 feet, Lorentz and Herrmann drifted classically west down the fall line. Too spent to go on, Herrmann collapsed in the snow. Lorentz tried to shelter his friend with packs and snowshoes before trudging on in search of Timberline Lodge. Neither heard the new foghorn at the lodge, which sent out a blast every fifteen minutes, nor saw the 1,000-watt searchlight that had been installed at the top of the Magic Mile ski lift just the day before. When searchers found Lorentz two days later, alive but hypothermic and snow blind, he was west of Paradise Park, six miles away from Timberline Lodge. A day later, they found Herrmann's frozen body—"head bare, hands bare, thumbs clenched in fingers in a futile effort for warmth," according to the *Oregonian*—just fifty yards from the edge of Mississippi Head.

ONE OF THE MOST heartbreaking tragedies on Hood also involved a South Side descent in horrendous weather conditions. But the climbers involved didn't stray west in the Mount Hood Triangle on their way down, and when they were found four long days after they'd set out to climb to the summit, they were on the western edge of White River Canyon at about 8,500 feet—within eyesight of Timberline Lodge.

At 2:30 a.m. on Monday, May 12, 1986, a team of climbers from the Oregon Episcopal School (OES), a private Portland school, set out from Timberline Lodge in decent but cold weather. A nasty bout of spring weather had been forecast for the region, prompting professional guide services like Rainier Mountaineering and Timberline Mountain Guides to cancel their climbs for the same day, but the OES outing proceeded as scheduled. The team included fifteen high school students, most of them fifteen-year-old sophomores who were enrolled in the school's Basecamp Wilderness Education Program. Also along: Father Tom Goman, a teacher at OES and climb leader who'd made the summit of Hood some fifteen times; Ralph Summers, a professional climbing guide; and a parent and a teacher.

The parent, Sharon Spray, who'd climbed the mountain before, and her daughter, Hilary, turned around within the first hour when Hilary became sick. Ten years after the climb, Spray told Tom Hallman Jr., a reporter for the *Oregonian*, that by the time they turned around, the weather had already deteriorated to the point of near whiteout. The rest of the team, however, powered on and made Silcox Hut in about two hours, double the time it takes most climbers.

"My lasting image is those kids walking past us, disappearing into the falling snow," Spray told Hallman.

Several more turned back before the top of the Palmer ski lift, but Goman reportedly and uncharacteristically pressed the remainders to buck up and push for the summit despite worsening weather. The group struggled through the weather and made it to the Hogsback, about a thousand feet below the top, sometime after 2:00 p.m.—nearly twelve hours after departing Timberline. On average, teams make it to the top in half that time.

With students, Goman, and the teacher, Marion Horwell, faltering, and 60 mph winds whipping up a bone-chilling whiteout, the decision was made to turn around. The climbers stopped for nearly an hour on the way down to try and warm hypothermic student Patrick McGinnis. Lost and disoriented after descending farther, Summers decided the party should dig in for the night, so he set to work excavating a snow cave for the team. Giles Thompson, one of the sophomores on the climb, later likened the cave to a single bed crammed with thirteen people.

Over the next three nights, three of the students would perish after leaving the cave and not making it back in. Summers and a student, Molly Schula, set out for help after the first night, wandering into Mt. Hood Meadows ski area the next morning. When rescuers finally found the buried and frozen cave on the fourth day, within fifteen feet of an area they'd searched repeatedly and just twenty minutes before the search effort was to be called off for good, only two people were left alive: Thompson and fifteen-year-old Brinton Clark. Both endured weeks of hospitalization; doctors also had to amputate both of Thompson's lower legs. His core body temperature when rescuers pulled him from the cave had been seventy-one degrees.

The school later suspended and then altered the Basecamp Wilderness Education Program and settled with all but one of the families. It also took a $500,000 hit from a wrongful death lawsuit filed by the parents of Richard Haeder, one of the students who died. Summers never spoke to the media. Clark, who went on to medical school, married, had a family, and returned to Portland to join the general medicine faculty at Providence Health & Services, did once. She told Hallman, who felt she'd anticipated his every move during their interview ten years later, that what happened on Mount Hood was a single element in her life, but not one that defined who she became. Thompson went on to become an accomplished skier, a father and husband, and an artisan for a theater company in Seattle. He drew a picture of the cave for Hallman, told him he'd never forgotten what it sounded like from in there, and that, with his life, he was just trying to make the most of the opportunity that he'd been given, and his classmates denied.

ANDREW CANFIELD stood out among the happy-hour folks milling about the Portland Staybridge Inn's courtyard one sunny summer evening in 2010. Tan and athletically sinewed, he was sitting at an outside table with a pale twentysomething who'd never heard about what happened on Mount Hood—and to Andrew Canfield—on May 30, 2002.

"Generally when I talk to people about it, it's like 9/11 or something," said Canfield, thirty-seven. "People remember exactly where they were when it happened. You get this mind imprint, I guess. But it's funny, these days a lot of younger kids don't know anything about it."

Canfield grew up in Chico, California, the fifth of nine children and one of the more adventurous. He was big into mountain biking and jumping from high places, like the train trestle sixty feet above the Feather River or from the towering cliffs above Big Chico Creek at a popular swimming spot known as Bear Hole.

"If I had nine lives, I probably used them all already," Canfield said.

Not interested in college or in whiling away his days at the town's glass repair company, he instead turned to the Air Force after graduation. His high school sweetheart was pregnant at the time, and because the Air Force wouldn't accept single parents, he walked out of the recruiter's office and proposed on the steps just outside.

During basic training, a group of Air Force pararescuemen, also known as PJs, made their pitch to Canfield and his fellow recruits. The PJs are the Air Force's elite special forces, somewhat akin to the Army's Green Berets or the Navy SEALs, though trained specifically to recover downed and injured aircrew, often in hostile environments and under fire. They jump from planes, dive in the ocean, climb mountains, save people, sometimes kill people. A childhood friend of mine, a major in the Army who worked with special operations forces in Colombia and Iraq, told me that if his plane ever crashed and he was wounded behind enemy lines, a PJ would be his first choice for a rescue.

After seeing the presentation, Canfield was hooked.

"I wanted to wear that maroon beret," he said of the service's trademark accoutrement. "It was the coolest thing in the world to an eighteen-year-old kid."

The young soldier aced the initial physical fitness test and went on to complete nearly two years of intense PJ training. The first eight weeks of the regimen include insane amounts of exercise, calisthenics, and swimming to winnow down a starting group of about a hundred recruits to just eight. The next year and a half sends PJs to various schools for training in everything from scuba diving and free-fall parachuting to field medicine, mountaineering, and a little course known as dunker training, where soldiers learn how to escape from a downed helicopter—underwater, upside down, and blindfolded.

In December 1994 Canfield graduated from PJ school and landed at Patrick Air Force Base on the east coast of Florida. His main charge: supporting space shuttle missions, particularly if a crew ever needed to be recovered from the ocean. One of Canfield's closet friends from PJ school, Jason Kutscher, took an altogether different assignment in Okinawa, Japan, one that Canfield himself had considered. Six months later, Kutscher was killed in a helicopter crash in South Korea.

"That was my first real clue that helicopters were dangerous," Canfield said.

※

ON THE CLEAR, blue morning of Thursday, May 30, 2002, William Ward, Richard Read, Harry Slutter, and Christopher Kern were picking their way down from the summit of Mount Hood through the Pearly Gates on the mountain's south side. A few hundred feet below the rope team was another descending and tied-together pair, John Biggs and Thomas Hillman. And just a little farther down, Jeff Pierce, Jeremiah Moffitt, and Cole Joiner were climbing up the Hogsback toward the summit, also tied into a rope and just above the bergschrund.

Sometime around 8:45 a.m., in exceptionally icy conditions, Ward slipped, landed on his back, and began sliding down the mountain, dragging first Read, then Slutter, then Kern along with him. The tangled mess snagged Biggs and Hillman and then the team of Pierce, Moffitt, and Joiner. All together they slid down the slick slope of the Hogsback and plunged twenty-five feet into the maw of the bergshrund.

Just before that fateful first slip, another climber far down below had used a telephoto lens to snap a photograph that showed almost all the involved rope teams in their respective positions on the Hogsback. The picture also revealed that the route at that time of the morning was still socked in shade, which made for an especially icy slope. The climber who made that photo was Steve Boyer, the doctor who'd been on the mountain when Tena and Carey Cardon had fallen. Boyer had set out to climb the mountain that day to keep an informal string of monthly climbs alive. According to his own records, by the time the streak ended he had climbed Hood every month for forty-three months in a row.

That morning he'd ridden to the top of the Palmer ski lift and started his solo climb. Because the slope was so icy that morning, he put his crampons on at 8,700 feet, lower than he ever had before. When Boyer took that first picture, he didn't think anything of it. Not until he rounded Crater Rock and approached the Hogsback did he find out that something was amiss.

"As I was approaching," he said, "someone told me that I was about to walk into a disaster."

AFTER THREE YEARS of work supporting the space shuttle missions in Florida, Andrew Canfield signed up for a tier one assignment that took him on adventurous missions overseas, including hunts for Osama bin Laden in the years before 9/11.

"It was like chasing a ghost," Canfield said.

But after four years of familial absence, the PJ's wife, who'd been home alone raising the couple's children, had had enough.

"She said either get your ass home or I won't be here when you do," Canfield said.

So he left active duty in August of 2001, just a month before the 9/11 attacks, and became a full-time reservist with the Air Force. The gig brought him and his family to Sandy, Oregon, a small town of just over 7,000 people that sits about halfway between Portland and the western flanks of Mount Hood. Situated as such, Canfield could be a part of the 304th Rescue Squadron of the Air Force Reserve Command's 939th Rescue Wing in Portland and yet live in the peaceful air of Sandy.

On the morning of May 30, 2002, Canfield reported for duty with the 939th like any other day. Crews were watching the news about the accident up on Mount Hood when the call came in for one of the base's HH-60 Pave Hawk helicopters to head to the mountain. Canfield and six other soldiers suited up: pilot Captain Grant Dysle, co-pilot Captain Kelvin Scribner, flight engineer Sergeant Martin Mills, combat rescue officer Second Lieutenant Ross Willson, Staff Sergeant Darrin Shore, and Tech Sergeant Anthony Reich, the latter three of whom were pararescue jumpers as well. At the time, they'd all been excited to take part in a mission up on Mount Hood.

"All the other guys who were watching us fly off were like, 'You sons a bitches,'" Canfield said.

UP AT THE BERGSCHRUND, a full-blown rescue was under way. Those who'd fallen into the crevasse may have been in bad shape, but they couldn't have asked for a choicer team of bystanders to be on hand to help. Boyer, an emergency room doctor for twenty-three years, reached the scene just before 10:00 a.m. to find that a pulley system to rescue those in the crevasse had already been set up. Another rope team who'd been on the downhill side of the bergschrund when the accident happened included two firefighters, the assistant fire marshal from Tualatin Valley Fire & Rescue (TVFR), and a paramedic from Metro West Ambulance. They had been part of a larger party that included the now-submerged rope team of Joiner, Pierce, and Moffitt. Both Pierce and Moffitt were themselves firefighters with TVFR, and Cole Joiner was the assistant fire marshal's fourteen-year-old son. Search and rescue personnel from Timberline Professional Ski Patrol, American

Medical Response, and Portland Mountain Rescue began arriving within the first hour.

Boyer descended into the crevasse to find a clutter of bodies and gear. Slutter and Pierce had already begun trying to help those around them who'd also fallen in. Read, Ward, and Biggs were dead.

The focus quickly turned to getting the survivors out of the chilly crevasse and off the mountain. Hillman had fractured ribs; Kern was hypothermic; Moffitt was battered, bruised, and had possibly punctured a lung. Soon after all the surviving climbers were out of the crevasse, a UH-60 Black Hawk helicopter from the 1042nd Medical Company of the Oregon Army National Guard in Salem arrived and began ferrying the most-seriously injured climbers off the mountain. The bird first flew Kern down to Timberline Lodge and an awaiting second Black Hawk. Running low on fuel, the pilot then plucked Hillman from the Hogsback and headed straight for Legacy Emanuel Medical Center in Portland.

That left only Jeremiah Moffitt—and the Pave Hawk, which was waiting down below at Timberline.

A MODIFIED VERSION of the Black Hawk, the Sikorsky HH-60 Pave Hawk was designed primarily for Air Force combat search and rescue missions. It varies from the Black Hawk mainly in the kind of onboard systems it's equipped with, as well as its in-flight refueling probe. At 22,000 pounds, Pave Hawks are also several thousand pounds heavier than Black Hawks.

When the call came to head up and retrieve Moffitt, the helicopter took off from Timberline. The crew made some calculations regarding the power needed to carry out the rescue in the thinner air at 10,000 feet, shed some of the helicopter's fuel to help lighten the load, and sailed up the mountain. Canfield sat next to Mills at the right door, which was open for the hoisting operation. Both were tethered to the helicopter by three-and-a-half-inch-wide gunner's belts.

The plan was to lower one crew member, Anthony Reich, to the Hogsback to help package Moffitt in a litter. In a complementary headwind, the helicopter drifted into a solid hover above the accident scene, dropped Reich down on the hoist, and circled back to await the ready signal.

"It was perfect," Canfield said.

After about five minutes, Moffitt was ready to be hauled up. The Pave Hawk eased back into a hover over the rescuers and climbers down below. Mills lowered the hoist, Reich attached it to the litter, gave the thumbs up, and the Pave Hawk started to lift, just enough to tighten the line.

"And then," Canfield said, "the bottom just dropped out. You felt it in your stomach. I've been in a lot of helicopters, and I knew this wasn't good. I knew we were going down."

At the same time, thirty feet below on the Hogsback, Boyer realized something wasn't right. All of a sudden, the sound of the helicopter changed dramatically and it started to sink.

"I said, 'Oh my god. It's going down,'" Boyer said.

A shift in the wind high up the mountain and a miscalculation of the necessary power slowed the helicopter's main rotor. The pilot hesitated to see if it would regain speed. It didn't, and in an instant, the tail of the falling Pave Hawk swung out away from the slope, the nose dropped, and the fuel probe and rotor blades smashed into the mountainside, shattering and scattering across the snowy slopes. Like an avalanche of snow and steel, the helicopter rolled down the mountain in a violent 800-foot tumble that left a trail of debris in its wake.

Inside, just as the helicopter was beginning to reel, Martin Mills hit a switch that sheared the cable connected to Jeremiah Moffitt down below, likely saving the injured climber's life but leaving himself tied to the helicopter. Canfield immediately unclipped from his tether, thinking he would jump out the open door and hit the snow thirty feet below. But as the helicopter swung around, that thirty-foot drop became more like seventy. Canfield hit the deck and experienced a blink of silence before the *Boom! Boom! Boom!* of helicopter meeting mountain.

Tossed around with gear and the other crew members like popcorn kernels, Canfield managed to wrap his arms around Darrin Shore and hang on. But the force that accompanied each successive role down the mountain stretched Canfield to the breaking point. Meanwhile, Martin Mills, still tethered by his gunner's belt, flung around like a fish on a line. By the third roll, he was out the door, twice steamrolled by the helicopter before the webbing finally broke and left him behind. On the fourth flip, Canfield could cling no more. He was shot out the door like a rag doll and immediately started barrel rolling down the snow. He remembered thinking, *Yes! I'm out!* before realizing that the Pave Hawk was above him—and rolling downhill faster than he was.

The helicopter caught up with Canfield, plowed over him— "It sounded like a freight train," he said—and came to a pounding rest after two more somersaults at the base of Crater Rock, 800 feet below the original accident site.

꿍

WITH HIS MEDICALLY inspired worldview, Boyer's reaction to
the aerial spectacle he'd just seen was decidedly practical.

"It happened so fast, and then it was over," he said of having just watched an eleven-ton aircraft careen down the side of a
mountain just a few hundred feet away. "Then we realized we had
a second rescue to take care of and six more injuries—or fatalities."

Jeff Livick, a member of Timberline's Professional Ski
Patrol team who was working his last shift of the season that day
and had been responding to the climbing accident, immediately
skied down to find Martin Mills stunned but alert and sitting
up in the snow. Mills had a broken ankle and wrist, a slight lac-
eration of the liver, and some neck and back pain. Boyer wanted
him flown off the mountain, but Mills staunchly refused, saying he never wanted to be in a helicopter near a mountain again.
Rescuers skied him down in a sled instead.

Canfield, too, was able to sit up immediately after being
crushed into the softening snow by the Pave Hawk. He watched
the helicopter continue its tumble, and when it all stopped, his
very first thought was, *I gotta get those guys out of there.* But the
second Canfield stood up, an immense pain washed over him.
Thinking his neck might be broken, he sat right back down and
watched Dysle, Scribner, Willson, and Shore climb from the
wreckage practically uninjured and signal that they were, somehow, OK. When Shore reached Canfield, the two exchanged pro-
fanities of disbelief and sat on the snowy slope laughing in uneasy
amazement that they were all alive.

In addition to the incredible pain in his neck—it wasn't
broken, but the muscles had been severely damaged—Canfield

had several cuts and bruises and the helicopter's engines had burned his head as it rolled over him. Otherwise, he was in decent shape, considering what he'd just been through. Boyer examined him and, worried about a rough sled ride down the mountain, suggested a helicopter evacuation for Canfield. Late that afternoon, two Black Hawks flew up and took Canfield and Moffitt to the hospital in Portland without incident.

Boyer, seeing no reason to end his monthly streak just yet, hoofed it on up to the summit. He took several photos of the accident scene from above, climbed back down to the bergschrund, then clipped into his skis for the ride back to Timberline.

THE DAY HAD BEEN ONE for the books on Mount Hood, the worst accident since the OES tragedy nearly two decades earlier. Three climbers were dead and six were injured; three helicopter crewmen were in the hospital. And a $13 million Air Force helicopter lay battered and upside down a thousand feet below the summit of the mountain with close to $5 million in damage.

The Forest Service closed the mountain to climbing for just over a week while the Air Force conducted an investigation and assessed the damage. Eight days after the accident, an Army Chinook helicopter lifted the Pave Hawk off the mountain in a giant sling and flew it to the nearby White River Sno-Park; from there, it was trucked back to the Air Force base in Portland. A few months later, the Air Force pointed its finger at the helicopter's crew for making several avoidable errors that led to the crash, including miscalculating the power needed and underestimating shifting winds. It also, however, commended the soldiers' eagerness to help and the pilot's efforts to guide the plummeting helicopter away from the crowded slope below.

The following year, on May 30, six of the climbers who'd been part of the accident and rescue climbed to the summit of Hood in part as a tribute to Ward, Read, and Biggs. With lightning bolts from an approaching thunderstorm visible to the south, they scattered some of Read's and Ward's ashes from the summit before heading back down.

BOYER MADE ANOTHER trip to the summit about a year later, this time with Andrew Canfield, who was glad to meet the doctor under slightly better circumstances than their first encounter. Canfield moved on fairly quickly after the crash, returning to his job after just four weeks. His first helicopter flight brought back intense memories of the accident; the aggressive motion of the flight also made him sick—something that had never happened to him before.

After the Hood incident but before he became a traditional reservist, Canfield deployed to places like Djibouti, Africa, and Iraq, where he helped rescue survivors of the massive bombing of the United Nations headquarters in Baghdad in 2003. He also plucked people from their roofs in New Orleans during Hurricane Katrina in 2005, convincing one schizophrenic man to override the voices in his head and leave his flooded home. Canfield has had intense, near-death experiences before—including falling twenty-five feet to the ground while fast-roping out of a helicopter in 1998—but what happened on Mount Hood has stayed with him like little else.

"There's definitely a psychological side that goes along with an experience like that," he said. "For me, sitting on the mountain immediately after that crash, all I could think was that I am so lucky to be alive. It was thankfulness for being alive, for my wife, for my kids, for my life, for the beautiful world, for just being able to breathe the air."

LOST

How does it feel to see Death in the flesh,
come to gather you in?

—Don DeLillo, *White Noise*

SOMETIMES THE TRACKS in the snow tell the whole story.
A skier heads out-of-bounds from the western edge of
Timberline's ski area. The rolling terrain over there, on the way
down into Sand Canyon and Little Zigzag Canyon, is simply
killer. Follow his tracks down a few hills, then a few more. Good
times. Now the tracks cut up a ridge and then back down. And
again. Maybe here, down farther than he'd expected to go, a little
worry begins to sink in. He turns around for the climb back up,
then intersects with his original tracks. Or are they? Around and
around he goes. And then, with the realization that he's been following his own tracks in circles for who knows how long now, he
drops to his knees.

Jim Tripp read more than a few of these ski-track sto-
rylines in his twenty-seven years with Timberline's Professional
Ski Patrol on Mount Hood. Now part of the host crew at Silcox

Hut, Tripp is a former Marine who used to teach soldiers at the corps' Mountain Warfare Training Center in Pickel Meadow, California. When he talks about skiing on Hood, whether on the round-the-mountain traverse above 7,000 feet or blasting 9,400 feet down the Leuthold Couloir and the north face of Yocum Ridge—"It holds powder like Canada," he said—Tripp lights up like someone who truly relishes life on the mountain. In 2000 he logged 272 days on the snow.

"With ski patrol you're in ski boots so much that your feet just get worked," he said. "But after all those years, I still love crankin' a good turn."

When a skier gets lost up at Timberline—heads down into Sand or Little Zigzag Canyons and starts wandering in circles, for example—Timberline's ski patrol and volunteers from the nation's oldest ski patrol, the Mt. Hood Ski Patrol, are usually first to head out on a search. In his days with the patrol, Tripp helped find a few desperate souls by following their tracks as they headed away from the resort. One guy they found was in the early throes of hypothermia and had begun to strip his clothes off. Another had been missing for a few hours, and when Tripp found him, he offered up a plastic cup of pudding. The hungry skier immediately tore off the lid and shoved it in his mouth.

"That guy was lucky," Tripp said. "He told me he'd felt death creeping in."

EVERY YEAR, people run into trouble around Mount Hood. With nearly five million annual visitors to the Mount Hood National Forest, including a million skiers, 67,000 wilderness users—among them 10,000 climbers—and 300,000 campers, it's no surprise. A little boy takes a wrong turn heading back to camp. A skier breaks his leg coming down the Tilly Jane trail. A pilot crash-lands on the Newton Clark Glacier and spends a cold and lonely night out in the wild. A young snowboarder suffocates upside down in a snowy tree well near Mt. Hood Meadows. Three climbers dare a winter weather window on Cooper Spur and are never seen alive again.

It's been happening throughout Hood's recorded history, from the oozing blood of William Travaillot on Dryer's climbing party to a soldier lost and never found at timberline in 1883, and from the OES tragedy and the Pave Hawk crash to the broken ankle of a climber who'd tried to summit with Yaktrax shoe chains strapped to his city boots in the summer of 2010. In 2007 a woman who had been hiking across the Muddy Fork of the Sandy River was pinned for more than six hours by a one-ton boulder after it rolled onto her foot. An Air Force B-26 bomber crashed into Mississippi Head in 1949. And three teenagers from Walla Walla, Washington, got stuck in a relentless blizzard up near Illumination Rock during a New Year's Eve climb in 1976. They spent sixteen socked-in days on the mountain, thirteen of them in a snow cave, but managed to survive until the weather broke and let them walk down to the top of the Palmer Snowfield and a search crew. Their prior week's rations had consisted of spoonfuls of Jell-O pudding powder and pancake mix.

And because people regularly run into trouble on Mount Hood, other people turn out to help.

Although recreational clubs like the Mazamas, the Snowshoe Club, and the Trails Club of Oregon had been exploring the mountain and its surrounds and helping with search and rescue since the turn of the twentieth century, an official search and rescue organization didn't exist on the mountain until a colorful and hardy bunch of climbers around Hood River made it official in 1926. Known as the Crag Rats—a name coined by the wife of one of the men—the volunteer group was initially a loose association of aficionados who found themselves involved in a number of searches for lost little hikers in the mid-1920s. After the Hood River contingent found missing seven-year-old Jack Strong below Yocum Ridge in 1926, they organized the club under the Crag Rats name, making it the oldest volunteer search and rescue organization in the entire United States. It's also the only one to have black-and-white checkered flannel shirts as their trademark garb.

"Some traditions are hard to shake," said Christopher Van Tilburg, a Hood River physician who has spent more than twenty-five years in wilderness medicine and a decade with the Crag Rats. "We don't wear 'em on rescues anymore, but you'll still see them around."

Unique in their attire as well as their longevity—membership includes three generations of some families—the Crag Rats also have an amazing clubhouse at their disposal: Cloud Cap Inn, high up on Hood's northeast side. The Inn, built in 1889, fell into disrepair over the years until—here we go again—the Forest Service thought about demolishing it in the early 1950s. In 1954 the Crag Rats petitioned the Forest Service for a special permit to use the building in exchange for restoring it, which they've done ever since.

The all-volunteer Crag Rats, about a hundred members total with twenty active rescuers, have responded to hundreds of incidents in their eighty-five-year history, everything from lost hikers and deceased mountain bikers to cliff jumpers, fallen climbers, and crashed planes. The Hood River County Sheriff's Office handles search and rescue missions throughout the area, including the north side of Mount Hood and the Columbia River Gorge, and calls on the Crag Rats about twelve to fifteen times a year. Members have also headed into impossible conditions to help with searches on the south side of Mount Hood.

On one such midnight mission in February 2007, Van Tilburg, who also works at the medical clinic at Mt. Hood Meadows Ski Resort, headed up to the edge of White River Canyon in a freezing snowstorm with 60 mph winds—so strong they knock you off balance—to help pinpoint the location of three climbers who'd fallen into the canyon. He and fellow Crag Rat Jeff Pricher used a mountain locator unit (MLU) to do just that. The locating device, developed after the OES tragedy and specific to Mount Hood, employs animal-tracking technology from the 1960s; climbers carry a rented transmitter, which sends signals when activated that rescuers can detect in the right conditions with a receiver.

Though rescuers located the climbers the next morning— thanks in part to the bearing the Crag Rats provided—and walked them off the mountain, a black Lab mix named Velvet got all the press. Tied in with the rope team that fell into the canyon, the hound took turns keeping the stranded climbers warm throughout the night. Within about a month of the ordeal, Velvet and her friends appeared on *The Ellen DeGeneres Show* and hosted a fund-raiser at the Lucky Labrador Brew Pub in Portland, all of which raised more than $50,000 for, among others, search and rescue teams like the Crag Rats.

❦

IN DECEMBER of 2006, Scott Norton was heading up the south side of Mount Hood inside a snowcat with a few other search and rescue volunteers from the well-known Portland Mountain Rescue (PMR). Their mission: to find three lost climbers who'd tried to climb Cooper Spur during a brief window of clear winter weather that had since closed in on them. Outside, it was fifteen degrees, and the winds and snow howled so fiercely that a few rescuers had to hop out and walk ahead so the cat driver could see where he was going. Rime ice, which collects in alluring patterns when tiny, supercooled water droplets encounter freezing cold objects like trees, cliffs, or parkas, grew on the rescuers like frozen stubble.

"We were slowly being absorbed by the mountain," said Norton.

So awful were the snow and wind conditions another day of the mission that Norton couldn't tell if he was moving on his skis or not. At one point during the descent from near Illumination Saddle, he started to lose his balance and stuck out a pole to steady himself.

"When my pole touched the ground," he said, "I realized I wasn't even moving. No idea how long I had been stopped."

They didn't find the three climbers—Kelly James, Brian Hall, and Jerry Cooke—that day. In fact no one ever found the latter two. But seven days after James had made a final call to his wife from inside a snow cave on Hood's north face, searchers poked through the ceiling of that cave and found his body inside.

A business systems analyst for Nike near its headquarters in Beaverton, Norton grew up hiking and backpacking in Idaho. He climbed Longs Peak in Colorado at sixteen and got into mountaineering big time when he moved to Oregon to work for Nike. Inspired by the video of the Pave Hawk crashing on Mount Hood and the rescuers on the scene, Norton hooked up with PMR in 2003 and has been an active member ever since. He was the organization's president in 2010.

One of several regional remnants of a statewide rescue group that fragmented in the early 1970s, PMR incorporated in 1977. Its all-volunteer, nonprofit makeup includes a hundred or so members, sixty of whom are field deployable. Sheriff's offices from three metro region counties call PMR for about twenty incidents every year. And while they'll do just about anything—they helped search for Kyron Horman, a missing eight-year-old who disappeared under mysterious and shady circumstances in the summer of 2010—their forte is high-angle, high-altitude rescue.

Most calls are for lost skiers or snowboarders, many of whom get lost in the wilderness adjacent to Timberline, and injured or missing climbers. Because so many climbing incidents happen on Hood's south side, PMR has even developed a signature rescue tool, the Hogsback Kit. It includes a lightweight 600-foot rope, anchors, and a stretcher, ideal for transporting injured climbers from the Hogsback to the top of the Palmer lift.

Like the guy who slapped Yaktrax on his boots, the climbers who get tripped up on Hood are often unprepared, uneducated, and lured up the mountain by a false sense of accessibility.

"It doesn't feel like a mountain wilderness, but it is," Norton said. "People come out, they're on vacation, maybe they rent an ice ax, maybe they don't."

One climber from Missouri took the north side's Sunshine route in 2001 without an ice ax, crampons, mountaineering boots, or helmet. He did, however, have a big bowie knife, which he used to cut steps in the ice. Though he made the summit, he got lost on his way down and took a mighty spill, triggering a rescue.

But ill preparedness or naivety is not always present when search and rescue crews head to the mountains. James, Cooke, and Hall, while they may have made some mistakes and pressed their luck, were considered experienced climbers. James had reportedly made climbs on Denali, the Eiger, and twenty-five or more on Rainier. Similarly, Luke Gullberg, Anthony Vietti, and Katie Nolan were considered seasoned climbers when they set out to climb Hood via the Reid Glacier Headwall during a slit of good weather in December 2009; Vietti was himself a member of Olympic Mountain Rescue. But the climbers ran into trouble. Nolan may have been injured, and when Gullberg descended for help, he fell. His body was found a few days later; searchers, including Norton, returned to the Reid the following August and found the bodies of Nolan and Vietti.

THE DRAMATIC NATURE of some of the search and rescue operations on the mountain makes for bold, attention-grabbing headlines that draw onlookers from far and wide. Gerald Herrmann and James Lorentz, the climbers who'd made the classic south-side descent error in 1940, were on the front page of the *Oregonian* for nearly a week straight, starting with the April 1 banner headline, "Two Men Lost in Storm on Hood" and ending with "Service Today for Herrmann" on April 6. In the digital and post–*Into Thin Air* age, climbing accidents get even more play. The helicopter crash on Hood in 2002 hit newscasts across the country and the world—how could it not?—and when James, Cooke, and Hall were lost in 2006, national media swarmed the scene like flies.

Of course, with all the attention paid to these incidents, everyone's suddenly a climber with an opinion. "To the sober person, adventurous conduct often seems insanity," wrote the late nineteenth-century German philosopher Georg Simmel, a sentiment amplified these days whenever climbs—and, it seems, only climbs—don't go as planned on Mount Hood. The second the search and rescue cavalry's called out, people start talking. Columnists and bloggers, many who've never strapped on a crampon, cash in their two cents from behind their keyboards. Online commenters respond in droves, particularly to stories that appear in the *Oregonian.* And people on the street feel compelled to ask questions and pass judgment like Monday morning quarterbacks who've never played the game in their life.

> *Why are they climbing in the winter?*
>
> *Why aren't they required to carry personal locator beacons?*
>
> *Who pays for the rescue up there? Why don't we send the climbers a bill?*
>
> *Why don't they close the mountain?*

Climbers chime in too, with don't-tread-on-me refrains about marring their wilderness experiences with mandates and how carrying beacons provides a false sense of security, encourages greater risks, and triggers unnecessary rescues.

"Oregon is a hotbed for that discussion because we've got one of the most-climbed peaks in the world," Van Tilburg said.

After the 2006 search for Cooke, Hall, and James, people from the Midwest called me to ask why in the world anyone would try and climb Hood in December. The answer is that if you time your window just right, Hood can be glorious to climb in the winter. Despite heightened avalanche and weather threats, the hordes of May and June are nowhere to be seen, a sizable hazard removed. The mountain in winter is also frozen solid, which helps reduce the threat of dangerous rockfall. And, if you ask me, someone who's never climbed the peak in winter and probably never will, Hood between late October and late spring, when the snow is fresh and the mountain stark white against an occasional clear blue sky, is at its absolutely most beautiful. All that said, there is no doubt that some climbers still make questionable decisions for winter attempts, trying to snatch the summit from tiny gaps in winter's frigid grip.

In the wake of climbing accidents, there's always well-intentioned talk of requiring climbers to carry personal locator beacons (PLB) or other signaling devices that in some cases might help rescuers locate lost or injured climbers more quickly. Advocates see it as a simple and inexpensive way (climbers can rent MLU transmitters for $5 a day from their local REI) to shorten lengthy and, as many believe, costly rescues. However, save for sheriff's office overtime and a few other expenses—and not counting the Pave Hawk crash—most rescues don't ring up huge bills. Most of the people involved are volunteers, and when the military sends out helicopters, the hours count toward monthly training requirements, so they're usually not out anything extra.

Lawmakers have even tried to enact laws along these lines. In 2007, just a few months after Kelly James's body was found, Oregon state representative John Lim introduced a bill in the legislature that would have required climbers to carry cell phones and either a GPS unit, a PLB, or an MLU above timberline between November and March. The bill passed in the House but never made it out of committee in the Senate. A similar law was in the pipeline in Washington State in the fall of 2010. Oregon also passed a first-ever law in 1995 that allows counties to bill people up to $500 for search and rescue services if they are deemed grossly negligent.

But mandating beacons garners stiff opposition from actual climbers and search and rescue personnel. Portland Mountain Rescue advocates them as one tool in a climber's arsenal, but would rather see people learn to use a map and compass properly and invest in training, good gear, and overall knowledge. Requiring people to carry beacons may imbue a false sense of security and lead climbers to take risks they normally might not. An over-reliance on technology can also lead to unnecessary distress calls. In the Grand Canyon in 2009, hikers with a beacon triggered helicopter rescues twice in two days, first because they were short on water and the next day because the water they did have tasted salty.

Norton said mandating anything also implies an endorsement of its effectiveness. So what happens if someone's mandated PLB doesn't work? And if you require a beacon, do you also, then, require a rescue on the other end? Even if Hall, Cooke, and James had been carrying a beacon, horrendous weather conditions prevented searchers from getting anywhere near the cave James was in for days. Is a climber who triggers his beacon entitled to a rescue even if searchers can't get to him?

But possibly the biggest point against mandating beacons is that, when it comes down to it, climbers don't run into that much trouble compared to many others who end up requiring search and rescue help. According to the Oregon Office of Emergency Management's most recent search report, there were 1,087 search and rescue missions in Oregon in 2009. Of those, nineteen were climbing related. The heavy hitters included game hunters (43), motor vehicles (131), and hikers (153). Search and rescue crews also responded to fifteen snowmobilers and sixteen mushroom pickers, none of whom seem to garner the attention that climbers on Mount Hood do.

OLIVER

O LIVER IS ABSOLUTELY *sprawled-out exhausted in the ashen dust of our campsite here at the base of Cooper Spur. The day has been a hot one, and long, and he knows little about conserving energy, at least not yet. Just a year old, the boy is every inch the black Labrador, boundless and happy and diving into life as only a dog can do. He's already got this signature spring going, whereby he leaps six feet straight up into the air from a complete standstill over and over and over again like a pogo stick so that he can see people over the backyard fence and out the front door. He prances around the house with socks in his mouth, slip-slides across the floor like a cartoon if he so much as hears the leash, and dashes around the backyard in what our vet once dubbed idiot laps whenever some unseen canine muse strikes. Oliver is also a natural trail hound who loves nothing more than a wide open romp in the wild—the expanse, the fresh mountain air and all its alluring scents, the chance to shed the tether and open up those long galloping legs the good lord's given him—capped off by a nice,*

*long snooze, preferably atop or even inside someone else's down
sleeping bag.*

*No doubt he doubled our miles and elevation from Cairn Basin
today, bounding ahead on the trail before racing back to us over
and over again. While we stop to take in the northern expanse—St.
Helens, Rainier, and Adams out over the Hood River Valley—he's
off chasing chipmunks; when we break among the bear grass at
Elk Cove with the mountain's north face looming overhead, Oliver
sniffs around and runs through the streams.*

*So by the time we get to our campsite tucked in between a
handful of massive boulders up above the Eliot Glacier near Cooper
Spur—after scoring some moleskin from a group of hikers crossing the creek down below—he's had it for the day. He thuds to the
ground in a cloud of gray dust, rolls over, and promptly conks out.
At beautiful sunset, he rises and sleepwalks his way into the tent for
what should be the rest of the night.*

But wait.

*Just as darkness sets in, the beast bolts from his dead sleep
and takes off up the mountain, baying like a wild coonhound. Amy
and I see nothing, hear nothing, and just assume he's caught the
scent of an animal in the breeze. Then, above the raucous barking,
a voice.*

*I dash off up the hill toward the barking and the screaming
and find that Oliver's treed himself a midnight hiker who happens
to be winding up a giant club of a walking stick for a swing at the
snarling black shadow in front of him. Luckily I get there just in
time. A blow from that club—and I can't blame the guy for almost
doing what he almost did—would have knocked Oliver silly and
probably ended our trek a couple days early.*

*Turns out he's a friendly local with a fancy for full-moon
hikes up Cooper Spur every year. Amy and I hadn't heard or seen*

him in the darkness working his way up the trail, but Oliver obviously had. I apologize to the guy, and by the time he resumes his stroll up the spur, he and Oliver are thick as thieves.

Later that night, after we've all faded away under the dark stars above Cooper Spur, Oliver throws out a couple random barks from atop my sleeping bag inside the tent. Must be the hiker making his way back down the mountain.

ICE

The glacier knocks in the cupboard,
The desert sighs in the bed,
And the crack in the tea-cup opens
A lane to the land of the dead.

—W. H. AUDEN, "As I Walked Out One Evening"

THE WORLD LOOKED DIFFERENT from inside a glacier: a bit cavernous and claustrophobic, the icy walls snow white and peppered with gray volcanic dust, and a hint of deep, dark blue down in the depths below. A bright but overcast sky kept me in touch with the above-ice world thirty feet overhead, but being down inside of Hood's largest glacier, the Eliot, didn't exactly impart a feeling of content or harmony. The muffled silence, accented by the occasional unseen trickle or shushing of loose snow somewhere off to a side, only added to the initial unease.

But it was amazing, too, to think about where I was and what I was doing—exploring the innards of an honest-to-goodness glacier, a massive sheet of ice that's been grinding its way down the mountain for millennia, chewing it up and regurgitating it down its namesake creek, on into the Hood and Columbia Rivers and, finally, into the Pacific Ocean; a glacier sundered by massive crevasses and saw-toothed with *seracs*, the towering, crumbling pinnacles that jut up from the ice when the entire mass itself fractures. Down in this one anonymous gash, tied in to a rope and belayed from a solid and purposeful anchor up above, I took in the tapering walls down below and on either side of me. I appreciated my vantage point for just a minute or two longer, then put the two ice tools in my hands to work and climbed back up out of the crevasse and into the bright and beautiful world above.

It was late summer, and seven of us had traipsed our way up the huge *moraine*—essentially a ridge of rocky debris deposited along the edges or terminus of a glacier—alongside the Eliot Glacier on Hood's northeast face. We found a jaw-dropping campsite among VW-sized boulders at the base of Cooper Spur and set up shop. We were there at the Eliot to do some ice climbing and practice crevasse rescue in part because a few of us were gearing up for a Mount Rainier climb the next season.

We spent the entire weekend hanging out on the glacier, crawling over its rocky debris, stepping over random runnels of meltwater, listening to it creak and slough. We built Z-pulleys to haul each other out of the ice and took long, lounging breaks to just soak in the giant mountain face behind us and the sprawling sheet of split ice all around. On the second day, Amy opted not to join us on the glacier and instead made the glorious day hike up to Tie-In Rock, where climbers rope up at the very base of the Cooper Spur route to the summit. At 8,500 feet, it's the highest and most dramatic day hike on the entire mountain, the closest feeling of actually climbing the beast without having to don crampons or an ice ax. From down on the Eliot, I watched her inch her way up the long ridge, silhouetted in the mountain's shade, and could not get the yodeling mountain climber from *The Price Is Right*'s Cliff Hangers game out of my head.

Along the Cooper Spur trail are three commemorations, one a subtle plaque among the high boulders in memory of mountain rescue pilot Robert Edling, who died in a crop duster plane crash in The Dalles in 1968. There's also a volcanic rock higher up on the spur informally known as Hiroshima Rock for the carved Japanese inscription on it dated July 17, 1910. The translated characters identify two visitors, one from Hiroshima and one from Mie Prefecture in Japan, but of their expedition, I could find little more. The third is a plaque on Tie-In Rock memorializing five Mazama climbers who were killed after a fall while descending Cooper Spur on June 21, 1981; on the very same day, eleven climbers died in a massive icefall on Mount Rainier in the worst mountaineering accident in US history. The plaque on Cooper Spur says, in part, "Walk gently, friend, you are walking in the path of those who went before."

When we made our Rainier climb the following August, thankful to be better-versed in our glacier rescue systems should anything happen, my eyes bulged at the sheer size of the crevasses on Rainier's Ingraham Glacier compared to those on the Eliot. One we skirted was more canyon than crack and looked like it could swallow a semi with ease.

RAINIER MAY HAVE CLAIM to some of the most notable glaciers in the lower forty-eight: the longest (nearly 6 miles) and thickest (705 feet) is the Carbon Glacier, and the largest is the Emmons Glacier, which at 4.3 square miles covers an area equivalent to about 2,100 football fields. The highest of all the Cascades, Rainier is home to twenty-three named glaciers, and boasts more glacial ice and snow—156 billion cubic feet—than all the other mountains in the range combined.

Hood, however, may be home to the first glacier ever officially "discovered" in the American West or at least described in scientific literature. Clarence King, a geologist charged by the US War Department with surveying western lands in 1867, sent Arnold Hague from San Francisco to study the volcanoes of Oregon and Washington. Hauge climbed Hood, checked out its glaciers, including the Sandy, and reported what he'd seen in a letter back to King in early September 1870. King, however, found a glacier while climbing Shastina, a sub peak of Mount Shasta in California, during the same time frame. He went on to publish his finding before Hague's, earning the credit for identifying the first glacier in the American West, even though the glaciers on Hood may have technically been tagged first.

Though some scientists use size to define a glacier, probably the simplest and most widely accepted definition is a mass of perennial snow and ice that moves. A glacier forms when snowflakes pile up and compress into a frozen mass that continues to gain more snow every winter than it loses water in the summer. Eventually the compacted snow becomes a huge block of ice, which then heads off at a snail's pace down the mountain. Similar to the mechanism behind ice skating, melting on the underside of a glacier creates a slick surface upon which the whole sheet can slide.

Most of the Cascade glaciers stem in part from the end of the last Ice Age, when massive ice sheets entombing the range began a long, slow retreat about 15,000 years ago. One notable exception: the Crater Glacier inside the Mount St. Helens crater, which formed in the wake of the 1980 eruption and grew rapidly until the volcanic unrest of 2004 nearly split the thing apart and slowed its growth considerably.

Mount Hood today, buried in about 40 feet of snow every year, is home to nearly 150 snow and ice bodies, including eleven true glaciers and one former glacier turned perennial snowfield. It all pushes the mountain's total volume of snow and ice to 12.3 billion cubic feet—143 billion less than Mount Rainier but nearly double that of the Three Sisters and almost triple that of Mount Shasta. The snowfield, called the Palmer after the pioneer trailblazer Joel Palmer, actually revealed itself to be a glacier during a low snow year in 1924. It was originally christened the Salmon Glacier after the river that flows from its toe, but two years later Lewis A. McArthur, compiler of the now-classic *Oregon Geographic Names*, petitioned the United States Board on Geographic Names to change it, saying simply that the current name was unsatisfactory.

Over the course of the twentieth century, however, the Palmer lost its mobility and so much of its volume that it's since been widely relegated to the lowly status of snowfield. Since the 1950s, it's also been home to many of the upper ski runs at Timberline. Operators there goose the snowfield every summer with close to a million pounds of salt to melt and refreeze its top layer for better skiing and boarding conditions, a practice that may be helping the Palmer linger longer than it otherwise might.

Like the Palmer, most all of Hood's glaciers bear the names of people with prominent ties to or involvement on the mountain. The 3.2-billion-cubic-foot Eliot Glacier honors Dr. Thomas Lamb Eliot, a late nineteenth-century Unitarian pastor in Portland with a penchant for mountaineering and spreading the good word about the glory of Hood. Eliot himself supposedly named the glacier next to his after a friend, Henry Coe, an early resident of the Hood River Valley who explored Hood's northern slopes in 1883 and later ran a coach line for mountain visitors. Coe tried to name another north side glacier after his own friend, Oscar Stranahan, in 1886, but the official name instead became Ladd, after William Mead Ladd, a Portland banker who built Cloud Cap Inn at 6,000 feet on the mountain's northeast corner. As for Stranahan, his name went to a lower forested ridge that separates the drainages of the Coe and Eliot Glaciers.

Also on the north face sits the small Langille Glacier, named after an intrepid nineteenth-century family from Nova Scotia that included Tantsana Langille, an early innkeeper at Cloud Cap, and her sons, William and Douglas, renowned mountain guides who pioneered climbing routes like Wy'east and Cooper Spur. On around to the west, the Glisan Glacier bears the name of Rodney Glisan, a paragon of civic activity in Portland in the late nineteenth and early twentieth centuries. His name also graces a street running through Portland, the pronunciation of which new arrivals to the city have a way of butchering. For the record, it's *GLEE-sin.*

Next comes the Sandy Glacier, whose primary stream, the Muddy Fork, joins the Sandy River proper six miles away. The Sandy River itself counts as its source the Reid Glacier, the centermost sheet of ice on Hood's western face when viewed from

Portland. Tucked in between the treacherous Yocum Ridge and an unnamed spine that trails down from Illumination Rock, the Reid takes its name from Harry Fielding Reid, a Johns Hopkins professor and glacial expert who urged the Mazamas to research the mountain's glaciers, which they started doing in the early 1900s.

The Zigzag Glacier shares a name with the river it spawns, and the White River Glacier, due east of the Palmer Snowfield, colors its namesake stream nearly white with *rock flour*—fine sediments ground into powder by the ice sheet. Above the White River Glacier and Crater Rock sits the highest and probably most-traveled glacier on all of Hood, the small Coalman Glacier. Home to the mountain's most notable crevasse, the bergschrund, the Coalman honors Elijah Coalman, a storied Mount Hood guide who first climbed the mountain at age fifteen in 1897 and over the next thirty-one years racked up a total of 586 trips to the summit. And the final face in the lineup, the Newton Clark, comes from a teacher and land surveyor of the same name who blazed a route to the summit up Cathedral Ridge in 1887.

ॐ

OF ALL THE THINGS to be smitten by in middle school—rock and roll, skateboarding, pretty girls—something else caught Andrew Fountain's fancy: snowflakes.

In the '70s, a scientist had come to Fountain's middle school in upstate New York and talked to him and his classmates about making and preserving snowflakes. Intrigued, Fountain later took to doing both as a hobby while in high school. Using a pan of hot water, he would create humidity in a box freezer, and then explode a bit of snap bead packing material inside it, which would spontaneously nucleate ice crystals into intricate, six-sided snowflakes. Wanting to pursue the crystals further in college, he was dissuaded instead toward physics by professors who told him if he studied snowflakes, he'd end up forecasting the weather during the eleven o'clock news.

Fountain went the physics route, including a study of lake ice during his senior year, chose cloud physics for his master's degree, and later earned his PhD in glacier hydrology from the University of Washington while working for the USGS and studying how water flows through glaciers. He's since researched glaciers in Alaska, Sweden, Antarctica—the USGS even named one after him in Antarctica in honor of all the work he's done to advance the science—and across the western United States, including on Mount Hood. In addition to teaching about glaciers and climate change as a professor of geology at Portland State University (PSU), Fountain has another area of interest these days: how glaciers melt.

WHEN I FOUND Fountain in his office at PSU, a Janis Joplin poster on his wall—apparently there's more to his background than snowflakes—he was decked out in a Cycle Oregon T-shirt, some black warm-up pants, and sandals. Turns out his father, a longtime employee of the phone company in New York who never really understood Fountain's geological pursuit, was wrong when he told his son that someday he'd have to grow up and wear a tie to work.

An engaging conversationalist with a knack for making talk of glacial geomorphology and the insulating properties of volcanic rocks not only understandable but also funny and fascinating, Fountain is one of just a handful of scientists who've looked closely at the glaciers on Hood. Despite its proximity to Portland, Hood is not the easiest place to study glaciers. Other than the Eliot, which can be a sketchy place to work because of potential rockfall, most of the mountain's glaciers take some pretty good slogs to reach. Additionally, curious hikers and climbers would likely not be able to keep their mitts off any scientific instruments set up on glaciers like the Coalman, along Hood's main climbing route, and the Eliot. Nonetheless, Fountain and a few of his peers and students have been looking at how the glaciers have shrunk since about a century ago, when the Mazamas first took some classic photos and measurements of Hood's ice sheets. His prognosis is not encouraging.

"The glaciers on Hood have probably lost a third to half of their volume since the turn of the twentieth century," he said.

And the culprit?

"It's for sure because of global warming. We've looked at changes in precipitation and temperature, and we can only explain the shrinkage of the glaciers due to global warming. And that's been consistent in all of our studies."

Over the past hundred years, the Northwest has warmed about a degree or so, according to the University of Washington's Climate Impacts Group. On Mount Hood, average summer temperatures have heated up from 42 degrees in 1902 to almost 48 degrees in 2002. That alone, according to Fountain and one of his former graduate research assistants, Keith Jackson, has been enough to downsize seven of Hood's largest glaciers an average of

34 percent. The Sandy Glacier has lost more than 60 percent of its area over the past century. The warmer temperatures naturally result in greater melting of the ice, but because Hood's glaciers are at relatively lower elevations, it also means that more of the mountain's precipitation has been falling as rain, not snow, and so the glaciers have been packing on fewer pounds every winter than they used to. The White River Glacier, a roughly mile-and-a-half-long sheet on Hood's southeastern flank, lost more than 1,600 feet of its length over the past hundred years in part because of climate change; it's also being hit higher up by geothermal heat escaping from vents around an area known as the Devil's Kitchen.

"It's getting hammered from above and below, so that glacier's days are numbered," Fountain said.

❧

ONE OF THE EASIEST ways to see just how much Hood's glaciers have retreated is to simply look at them. Thankfully, the Mazamas have long been interested in not only climbing and hiking, but in the science of the mountain as well. They established a research committee in 1924, whose first field trip was to pick up the study of the Reid Glacier where Reid himself had left off. Bad weather and poor visibility during that outing sent them instead over to a snowfield to investigate reports of never-before-seen crevasses. They found the cracks and confirmed that the snowfield was actually a glacier—the Salmon Glacier.

Throughout the early and middle parts of the twentieth century, the club studied and measured many of Hood's glaciers. One remnant of that work, besides all the data and reports stored within the club's archives, are a few random boulders in nearby moraines that were painted red and used to track movement back in the day. Apparently some of them are still kicking around up near the Eliot. The Mazamas also photographed many of the glaciers and in 1935 initiated an aerial photo survey of the mountain, all of which gives a good picture of what Hood's glaciers looked like up to a hundred years ago.

On a Friday night in spring 2010, I headed to the Mazamas headquarters in southeast Portland for a three-hour presentation on Hood's glaciers featuring not only Dr. Fountain, but also Karl Lillquist, a geography professor at Central Washington University. Lillquist used the Mazamas' glacier photos, along with other aerial shots he had purchased, as a baseline and went back and photographed the glaciers from roughly the same spots in 2001. He also had the benefit of GPS technology and other advances that earlier researchers did not. Through his research, Lillquist found that Hood's glaciers were on the retreat from about 1900 to the midcentury, when they actually began to advance for a few years. But by the 1970s, the retreat was on again—and has been ever since.

For many of the studied glaciers, putting the early twentieth-century photos next to those from 2001, as Lillquist did, is startling. In 1902 the White River Glacier cascaded down the mountain in a tremendous white blanket of ice, broad and full and thick. In the 2001 photo, however, it looks like a dirty hanky about half the size of its former self. Despite a brief advance of about 260 feet in the late 1960s, the Eliot Glacier receded more than 2,500 feet between 1901 and 2001. The 1901 photo shows the debris-strewn glacier nearly topping out of a deep trough; in the 2001 image the glacier has retreated so far uphill that it's not in the frame at all.

☙

It is not, however, easy to make a glacier disappear—despite what some in the media might say. A 1940 news article about the Dana Glacier in the central Sierra Nevada mountains of California predicted that the glacier could be completely gone within fifty years. In a photo from 2004, sixty-four years later, the Dana Glacier looks almost as stout and happy as it did back during Roosevelt's second term. That's likely because, as glaciers do retreat, they enter more favorable environments, higher up on mountainsides and into protected cirques where the temperature is colder and the snowfall and avalanching contributions to their mass are greater.

Along similar lines, Lillquist's study only measured the fluctuation in the termini of the Hood glaciers, not that of their thickness. According to Fountain, there are limited cases where a glacier can retreat and thicken or advance and thin. In addition, everything from a glacier's location and slope to the amount of debris covering it can also impact how glaciers advance or retreat. The lower portion of the Eliot Glacier, for example, is covered in rock debris that crumbles off the north face of Hood, catches a ride in the ice of the Eliot, and is eventually spit out farther down. The blanket of rocks actually helps insulate the ice and staves off at least a little bit of the melt.

Nonetheless, the glaciers on Mount Hood and across the American West—and really, around the world—are shrinking. According to Fountain, even though the melting on Greenland and Antarctica gets all the press, shrinkage of glaciers like those on Mount Hood is a major contributor to the slow rise of the seas.

"Other than the warming of the oceans, the addition of new water to the oceans will still be dominated by the small glaciers through the end of this century, so they deserve being paid attention to," he said.

On a more local level, the melting and retreat of the glaciers on Hood may already be making its presence known. As the ice sheets recede, there's little left to buttress the weak layers of volcanic debris in the valleys and canyons down below. The streams that flow from glaciers erode and weaken these valley walls to the point of near collapse. Throw in a good rainstorm and it's party time.

In November 2006 more than a foot of rain fell on Mount Hood in seven days. A huge amount of water likely ponded in the Eliot Glacier and then roared out, a geologic phenomenon known as a glacial outburst flood or *jökulhlaup*. The rush washed out the Timberline Trail's crossing of Eliot Creek—as of 2010, it had yet to be restored—trashed irrigation infrastructure in the Hood River Valley's Middle Fork Irrigation District, and rolled SUV-sized boulders down the channel. It also engorged the Eliot from a 150-foot-wide stream into a river nearly a thousand feet across, and built a new delta in the Columbia River at the mouth of the Hood River that, in an unexpected twist of good fortune, has since become a favored spot for windsurfers and kiteboarders.

Another flood during the same storm took out a key bridge over the Sandy River on Hood's west side, and high up on the White River, debris dammed the stream and then broke loose, sending more than a million cubic yards of boulders and mud and a million gallons of water down the valley. The torrent buried the riverbed under thirty feet of debris and the Highway 35 bridge across the White River on Hood's east side in six feet of rock and glacial detritus. A little farther north, Newton Creek and Clark

Creek jumped their channels and wrought similar havoc. The whole deal closed Highway 35 for more than a month, cutting off access to the Mt. Hood Meadows ski area from both the north and the south. It was the eighth time the highway had been closed in five years, the twentieth time since it opened in 1907. In the summer of 2010, road crews were hard at work raising the road-bed and installing new bridges over the river and huge twelve-foot and twenty-foot culverts nearby, all in a $20 million effort to blunt the blow the next time the White decides to give back.

"The glaciers definitely help maintain the edifice of Hood," Fountain said, "so we're going to see a lot more of that kind of thing."

SHRINKING GLACIERS on Mount Hood could also someday give up some ghosts that have long been lost. Pieces of weathered one-by-fours have appeared among the crevasses of the Eliot, likely the remains of the last summit cabin, which was abandoned in 1934 and reportedly collapsed ten years later. In other crevasses, Fountain has found old tin cans and abandoned scientific equipment from long-ago expeditions. Somewhere in a glacier in Alaska is a student of the National Outdoor Leadership School who fell down a natural glacial shaft known as a moulin. Fountain was working in the area when the sheriff's department contacted him to borrow his glacier drill and camera. Searchers scanned the glacier with another camera but never found the student.

People can be lost in glaciers for ages. In the summer of 2010, a melting glacier in the Canadian Rockies gave up the body of a Maine climber who'd fallen to his death twenty-one years earlier. Just two weeks after a friend and I had passed the shrinking Crescent Glacier during a climb of Mount Adams in 2001, another climber noticed a rope, then a boot, sticking out of the ice. Buried underneath were the bodies of Gary Claeys and Matt Larson, two climbers who went missing during a storm on the mountain in November 1980. Ice climbers also found the remains of a crewman from a US Army Air Corps plane crash in California's Mendel Glacier in 2005—sixty-three years after the plane went down. And in 1991 two German hikers happened upon a corpse frozen in a patch of stagnant ice in the Schnalstal Glacier in the Ötztal Alps of Italy. They originally thought the body was that of an unlucky climber from recent times. But Ötzie, as the mummified corpse was later named, turned out to be a 5,300-year-old Neolithic man who'd been shot in the back with an arrow.

Several climbers and hikers have gone missing on Hood and never been found. Chances are, they never will be, especially if they fell into a crevasse high up on a glacier. At these upper reaches of the glacier, where more snow accumulates than melts every year, the flow pattern tends to push objects—rocks, lumber, bodies—down deeper into the ice. If, for example, you fell into the bergschrund high up on the Coalman Glacier on Hood's south side and nobody pulled you out, you'd be slowly drawn to the bottom of the ice sheet and carried down the mountain along the glacier's underbelly. Fountain used the word "shearing" to describe what goes on down there. Austrian researchers investigating six bodies that emerged from glaciers in the Alps in 1991, including Ötzie, described it by saying that the same "tensile stresses" that cause glaciers to crack and form crevasses in the first place have a way of dismembering immersed bodies.

"There's a good chance you won't ever be recovered because of that," Fountain said.

But if you were to go in lower on the glacier in the ablation zone, where annual snow and ice melt surpasses accumulation, the flow pushes upward and there's less of that . . . shearing . . . going on—in which case there's a better chance that the glacier will eventually release you in a somewhat more recognizable form.

᠅

THE HOOD RIVER VALLEY in the northern shadow of Mount Hood is renowned for its pears, apples, peaches, cherries, and, more recently, wine grapes. Nathaniel Coe, a postal agent for the US government in the mid-nineteenth century, brought the first fruit trees to the Hood River area when he settled in what is now the city of Hood River in 1854. Apples originally took off, but a killer freeze in 1919 prompted most orchardists to switch to the hardier pear. Today the valley produces roughly 150,000 tons of pears, 8,200 tons of apples, and more than 29,000 tons of out-of-this-world cherries every year.

To produce such a bounty—the tree fruit, berry, and nut crop was worth $96 million in 2007—farmers use the Hood River to irrigate their crops, including more than twenty square miles of orchard land throughout the valley. The twenty-five-mile river begins its life as three separate branches running off of the northern and eastern bases of Hood: the East, Middle, and Upper Forks, all of them fed at least partially by melting water from glaciers like the Eliot, Coe, and Newton Clark. A team of Oregon State University Researchers, including Anne Nolin, an associate geosciences professor, studied the Upper Middle Fork of the Hood River in 2007 and found that glacial melt contributed anywhere from just under half to almost three-quarters of the streamflow of that fork during a typical August.

Five irrigation districts along these three main branches of the Hood River rely on summertime snow and ice melt to help slake the valley's agricultural thirst and provide cool, flowing water for threatened anadromous fish. Water from the glaciers is especially key in the late summer months, when the snow is largely melted, the rain is virtually nonexistent, and the harvest of nearly 160,000 tons of apples and pears across the valley begins.

The researchers noted that if temperatures continue to rise, the amount of runoff from the glaciers will increase too. While that may sound good for water users in the upper valley who divert water for irrigation and hydropower, there is another factor to consider—the continued shrinkage of the glaciers. The more a glacier's area shrinks, the less water pours off of it. As a result, based on the past hundred years of disappearing acts by glaciers like the Eliot, the amount of glacial meltwater that helped quench apple orchards a century ago is already markedly less than what's hydrating the valley's signature pears today.

FRAGILE ALPINE ecosystems high up on Hood, home to dwindling whitebark pine trees, scrubby wildflowers, and mammals like the mousy pika and chubby mountain woodchucks known as marmots, might also be dinged by retreating glaciers. Because peaks like Hood, Rainier, and Adams have been described as island geographies, subalpine plants and animals may simply have nowhere else to go once the snow and ice vital to their livelihoods retreats too high up the mountains' flanks or disappears altogether.

Thanks also to shrinking glaciers, most of the USGS maps that depict glaciers on Mount Hood are woefully inaccurate and out-of-date—to the point that they've nearly lost their utility in the high alpine country. Most of the quadrangles were originally made fifty or sixty years ago, and though they've since been updated, they don't take into account the dwindling glaciers. As a result, many climbing routes are no longer accurately represented on the maps because they often include sections of glacier that simply aren't there anymore. In the course of her study, Nolin found that the original USGS maps also inflated the area of some glaciers by including seasonal snowfields and deflated others by not including debris-covered sections.

One other corner of the Mount Hood world that could be impacted long-term by the retreat of the mountain's glaciers, or at least the forces causing it, is the ski industry. Hood is currently home to five ski areas: four on the mountain itself and one just across Highway 26 in the foothills. No one's forecasting the end of summer skiing on the Palmer just yet, though year-round skiing at Timberline is already a bit of a misnomer: the lifts actually close after Labor Day for a month or so, when there's seemingly more gray on the mountain than white. But Timberline can still boast the longest season in North America, and the snow is still bound to pile up by the hundreds of inches every year on the slopes of Skibowl and Summit, Mt. Hood Meadows and Cooper Spur for years to come. But after seeing what Hood's glaciers looked like in 1901 and what they look like today, a little apprehension is understandable.

"For the ski industry, it's all about how high the snow line can increase and still be viable," Fountain said. "I don't know what that is, but they're in danger for sure."

CLOSE

S O HERE WE ARE: *four days and about thirty-three miles into this five-day, forty-one-mile circuit around Mount Hood. Cooper Spur is long behind us; so is the aptly named Gnarl Ridge, a grotesque and steep serration up the mountain's east flanks that affords a bulky view of Hood rarely seen by those who keep to the Portland side of the peak.*

Just one day to go. But no.

We're done.

All those miles, the blisters, the aching knees, the sun and rain and sweat and tears, only to be turned back by what I swear is just a three-foot gap across Newton Creek, a high mountain stream that pours from the Newton Clark Glacier down the east side of Hood.

Only today the waters of this creek are not simply pouring; they are pounding their way down the mountain, gushing and churning and roiling.

Stout logs that once provided safe passage across the creek have been cast aside or submerged. The creek, so white at its snowy headwaters, is chocolate-milk brown with mountain silt, and it's tossing boulders about beneath its surface. It sounds like the ocean surf accented by bowling balls clacking down a bobsled run.

I admit, I am uneasy standing here looking at this monster.

But I could so very easily just take a long stride, maybe a small jump, and clear the void separating me from not only the far bank, but the last eight miles of the most classic hike in the state, a hike I may or may not ever get to try in its entirety again, one to tick off the life list. With a little assistance—and despite her obvious apprehension and silent, welling-eyed disagreement with my stubborn resolve—I even think Amy could bridge the gap.

But not Oliver. Sure, he's an inveterate swimmer and has all the energy and agility that comes stock with Labrador puppies.

But this water is too deep, too fast, and way too consequential if things don't go right. When I pull a heavy, eight-foot log up from the water's edge, its tip gets caught in the current and is swept from my grip. Amy's eyes drill into my skull and I know she thinks I'm an idiot for saying thanks but no thanks to the group of hikers who just offered us a ride back to our car at Timberline since we were about to bail just as they had. Then I think about Oliver putting one paw in the water, or slipping as we try to coax him to jump across, and the rush simply sucking him away, his eyes worried and helpless, his paws flailing, his head going under.

No way. It's just not worth it. We're done.

SAVINGS

*No, wilderness is not a luxury but a necessity of the
human spirit, and as vital to our lives as water and good
bread.*

—EDWARD ABBEY, *Desert Solitaire*

T HE HEADLINE in the *Oregonian* of Sunday, March 17,
2002, grabbed hold of my attention like someone screaming in my ear.

"Meadows Owners Plan New Resort on Mount Hood"

The proposal: up to 450 homes, hotel rooms, and condominiums; restaurants, a golf course, an ice rink, and—gasp—a retail
village, all of it not somewhere that's already been developed, like
Government Camp, but high up on the slopes of the wild north
side of the mountain, just below one of the most amazing alpine
escapes on all of Mount Hood, a place that I hold in true reverence:
Cooper Spur.

My friend Mark and I snowshoed up to Cloud Cap Inn near the base of Cooper Spur one February morning, when gray winter clouds smothered Portland. But high up at Cloud Cap, the skies were blue and clear. Hood's north face, Cooper Spur included, simply towered. We had the place to ourselves save for some Crag Rats who sat on the Cloud Cap porch around a silver barrel of beer.

We introduced a Cooper Spur camping spot among the high boulders to a group of friends a few years later, and they, like anyone who's lucky enough to experience it, were blown away. It's hard not to be. By the time you break out of the thinning hemlocks and firs above the Cloud Cap Saddle Campground, you're already well above the 6,000-foot level. We didn't go up to Tie-In Rock on that trip, but with views stretching from Mount Adams, Mount Rainier, and Mount St. Helens to the desert of Eastern Oregon and the crumbling Eliot Glacier right there on Hood's dramatic north face, we didn't need to.

I also spent the night up amongst those boulders with my dad, who at the time was sixty-two. That year marked our fourth in a row of overnight backpacking trips, which had taken us around Mount St. Helens on the Loowit Trail, up Old Snowy Mountain in the Goat Rocks of Washington, and to the top of the 10,000-foot Middle Sister in Central Oregon. At Cooper Spur, we enjoyed the relatively easy stroll up—just under two miles to our camp, as opposed to the ten-mile days we'd had on St. Helens—and then just relaxed with some of the most incredible alpine scenery expanding before us in every direction. The next morning we rose early to saunter up switchbacks and top out at Tie-In Rock at 8,500 feet. One of my all-time favorite pictures of my dad shows him relaxing at the base of Cooper Spur. There's

my dad, a lifelong Ohioan save for a four-year stint at Wesleyan
University in Connecticut, way, way up on Mount Hood.

So Cooper Spur, to me, has always been a truly majestic
place on the mountain.

The Meadows proposal wasn't the first one to visit the
Cooper Spur area. One from 1927 would have tastefully expanded
the existing Cloud Cap Inn, but two others in 1931 looked more
like monstrous urban apartment buildings. One even included
plans for a tram all the way to the summit of the mountain. A
positive outcome of the Great Depression: neither plan ever went
forward.

Meadows' proposed resort in 2002 would have been downhill a little ways from Cooper Spur, near the Cooper Spur Ski
and Recreation Area, a quaint little slice of the mountain that
grew from a one-hill ski jump in 1927 into a modest lodge, a few
cabins, and a ten-run ski area over the decades. Also nearby is the
nationally designated historic Cloud Cap–Tilly Jane Recreation
Area, which includes Cloud Cap Inn, the Snowshoe Club Cabin,
the Tilly Jane Ski Cabin, a scenic ski trail, and the old American
Legion Cook Shed, which the Legion once used for signature
annual climbs of Mount Hood.

At the time they made their plans public, Mt. Hood
Meadows had recently purchased the sleepy little Cooper Spur
Lodge and the lease for the Cooper Spur ski area. They'd also
been assembling land parcels in the area since the 1970s in anticipation of someday being able to bring overnight guests to the
mountain somewhere else besides Government Camp. Meadows
had tried to add lodging to its operations in the past but had been
repeatedly denied by the Forest Service.

And Kate McCarthy.

〜☙

BORN IN THE NORTHERN shadow of Mount Hood at the height of World War I, McCarthy grew up with the mountain, hiking its meadows, riding horses, skiing. Her father, Homer Rogers, ran their home as the Mount Hood Lodge and welcomed guests from Portland, who would ride the train to Parkdale and then come by wagon or sleigh up to the lodge. He also later bought and ran Cloud Cap Inn before selling it a few years later. Life, school, and marriage led McCarthy, who'd worked at Timberline Lodge on opening day, away from the mountain during some of her early adult days, but she returned to it full-time in 1968, and she's never left. She's climbed Cooper Spur, the South Side, and Wy'east, and, at a very spry ninety-three, was still hitting the trail.

"They're all my favorite," she said.

In the early days of fall 2010, I drove to the north side of the mountain once again, this time to meet McCarthy at her home in the Upper Hood River Valley above Parkdale. The first colors of autumn had already begun to seep into the leaves up there, and though the mountain was veiled in thin white clouds, I could see the first snow of the season on its dark outcrops through the wisps. McCarthy gave me a hearty hello before I even got out of the car. Dressed sharply in blue jeans and a flowered denim jacket, she shared with me piles of amazing old photographs—her father peering down a yawning crevasse on the Eliot Glacier, guests in front of Cloud Cap Inn, long lines of climbers making their way up Cooper Spur—and stories from her childhood.

McCarthy also talked about her long-standing efforts to try and preserve and protect Mount Hood. Upon returning to the mountain in 1968, McCarthy said she'd been flabbergasted with some of the environmental damage that had occurred in the fragile meadows and wetland areas when Mt. Hood Meadows was built. She was part of a citizens group that opposed rezoning the upper valley's farmland into one-acre home sites in the late 1970s and also Meadows' various plans for expansion over the years. The drawing for one of the plans included a golf course, with McCarthy's home right in the middle of it.

"At least they were nice enough to let us stay," she said, "though I'm sure all of our windows would have been broken."

In 1988 she formed Friends of Mount Hood as part of a successful effort to stop an expansion plan by Meadows that would have added 1,500 overnight units to its operations, many of them built in delicate wetlands within the Stringer Meadows. And when the ski resort announced its plans for the Cooper Spur area in 2002, McCarthy hit the road with a traveling slide show to convince people that the damage from such a resort on the mountain's north side, which ranged from increased traffic and pollution to harming the valuable Crystal Springs watershed, wasn't worth it. Some controversial backroom machinations by county commissioners, including a questionable land swap, didn't help the proposed resort's case much, either. In 2004, with the help of the nonprofit Crag Law Center in Portland, McCarthy and other county residents negotiated a settlement that nixed the resort, laid the groundwork for a land swap that would exchange Meadows' 770 acres on the north side for about 120 acres of prime development property in Government Camp, and will ultimately protect much of the Cooper Spur area.

"When all that's finalized, it will be a big deal," said Chris Winter, an attorney and one of the founders of the Crag Law

Center. "It will signal the protection of much of the Cooper Spur area as wilderness, which means forever."

THE COOPER SPUR issue represents some of what's in store for Mount Hood in the coming years. Portland and its metro region are proving to be an attractive draw to outsiders. And who can blame them? Mild climate, ocean sixty miles one way, beautiful mountain sixty miles the other direction, more breweries than any other city in the world. But the area's popularity will come at a cost. The population of the metro region is projected to double by 2060 to 3.8 million people. That means more visitors to Timberline Lodge, more climbers up the South Side, more skiers on the slopes, and more hikers at places like Zigzag Mountain and Elk Meadows. It also means more water being pulled from the Bull Run, more cars on the roads to the mountain and in the parking lots once they get there, and more strain on the parts of the national forest that people use most.

In 2010 RLK and Company at Timberline Lodge submitted to the Forest Service a proposal for lift-serviced downhill mountain biking, which would allow mountain bikers to hop on the Jeff Flood Express chairlift, throw their bikes on special carriers fitted to the lift, and ride down a fifteen-mile network of trails, some three feet wide, others six, over about eight acres. A separate skills park, not visible from Timberline Lodge, would eat up about an acre. The goal is to capitalize on the ski area's mountainous terrain during the summer months, much like the Whistler Mountain Bike Park in British Columbia.

Kate McCarthy and people of similar persuasion were not happy.

"Mount Hood is such an important treasure, I just don't see ruining it any more," McCarthy said, expressing fears that mountain bikes will trash fragile meadows, crisscross old-growth forests, and deprive hikers of access to the area. Opponents also note that just across the way at Skibowl, forty miles of lift-serviced bike trails already exist.

But Timberline makes its case as well, as do mountain bikers, many of whom take umbrage when National Forest lands become off-limits to them through wilderness designations. For Timberline, it's all about being careful with any trails they may build, meeting demand, and also managing the recreation that happens on the mountain.

"Having developed recreation and allowing the masses to use site-specific locations allows other places to remain pristine," said Timberline's Jeff Kohnstamm. "The ski areas take a lot of flak for development, but at the same time, we serve a large amount of people with a known impact—and a manageable one."

Another pressure on the mountain and its surrounding environment has come from the realm of energy. Environmental groups like Bark have been watchdogging plans by utility companies such as Portland General Electric (PGE) and NW Natural to further utilize portions of the Mount Hood National Forest as energy transmission corridors—for liquefied natural gas pipelines and other power sources—and geothermal energy. PGE, for example, has expressed interest in exploring certain areas around Mount Hood for geothermal resources. Amy Harwood, a program director with Bark, said the idea of geothermal energy—basically harnessing natural heat sources like underground volcanic activity to produce electricity—is widely accepted around Portland until people realize where PGE wants to look: near Tamanawas Falls, a gorgeous waterfall at the northeast base of Hood.

"It's amazing to me how people have found that one spot on Hood that is really important to them," Harwood said. "People are for renewable energy sources like geothermal, but then they hear it's at Tamanawas Falls and their view changes."

⌇⌇

THERE ARE, HOWEVER, a few areas on and around Mount Hood that are never going to see gas pipelines or new condominiums; a few more hikers maybe, but that's about it.

Wilderness.

Before 2009 the Mount Hood National Forest was home to just under 200,000 acres of federally designated wilderness, the highest level of protection that any piece of land in the country can receive. While that may have been plenty for some in the timber industry and the biking and ATV circles, for many Oregonians, it wasn't enough.

Eric Fernandez, wilderness coordinator for the conservation group Oregon Wild, started working on the idea of increasing the wilderness acres on Mount Hood and across Oregon in 1997, when he first started volunteering with Oregon Wild. Back then, his main duty was a GIS mapping project that identified all the areas across the state that would qualify for wilderness protection, including lands around Mount Hood. In 2003 a more formal campaign for new wilderness areas kicked off. It included 170,000 acres in the Mount Hood National Forest. When I asked Fernandez, who is soft-spoken but direct, where the initial proposal originated, he only half-jokingly pointed to his unassuming office down a dark hallway at the Oregon Wild headquarters.

Of course, other conservation groups like the Sierra Club and Friends of the Columbia Gorge were also involved, as were federal lawmakers like Oregon senators Ron Wyden and Gordon Smith, and Oregon congressmen Pete DeFazio, Earl Blumenauer, and Greg Walden. Unfortunately, a senator from Oklahoma, Republican Tom Coburn, a notorious road blocker in Congress, also got involved with the wilderness proposal. Coburn single-handedly held up the wilderness legislation for years, decrying it as little more than Oregon pork.

But in March of 2009, with the original wilderness proposal winnowed down to 127,000 acres around Mount Hood—200,000 acres across the entire state—lawmakers finally got around Coburn and hooked the wilderness provision onto a massive omnibus bill. President Obama signed the bill on March 30, 2009, granting permanent protection to lands around Mount Hood, from Eagle Creek and scenic Mirror Lake, with its spectacular view of Hood, to Elk Cove and 300 acres near Cloud Cap. The Mount Hood National Forest now includes more than 315,000 acres—roughly 30 percent of the entire forest—of designated wilderness.

The only shortfall in the eyes of those who advocated for greater protection? The fact that Bonnie Butte, Boulder Lake, the Salmon River keyhole, and a few other areas didn't make the cut this time around.

"Once this became law, we celebrated for about five minutes," Fernandez said. "Then we said, 'We're not done. We've got a lot more work to do.'"

DONE

I'M SO DEFLATED. *I don't want to talk to Amy on the way back down the trail. She justifies the decision to turn around at Newton Creek in any number of ways, and while I know she's probably right, I hear only a blur of words as the Timberline Trail slips away from me. So close to such a monumental feat, at least for an Oregon hiker, and we're going to fall short. I did not plan on this whatsoever. We were to knock this stroll off the list in five glorious days and get on with it. Maybe we'd get the chance to do it all again sometime later, but if we didn't, what would it matter? We'd have already done it.*

Nope.

Instead, we're going to say we've done three-quarters of the Timberline Trail, thirty-three of its forty-one miles, but we had to turn around because one gush of glacial melt just wouldn't let us pass. Not quite the same ring to it.

Our plan B is to backtrack and hike two miles down to Elk Meadows for the night. It's beautiful there, sure: a wide-open meadow with an unbelievable view of Hood's broad east face. Nothing to complain about, but I don't want to camp there tonight, and I sure as hell don't want to wake up tomorrow morning and hike out to Highway 35 so I can thumb a ride back to Timberline Lodge. Humiliating as it is, that's the plan.

But then we start tapping into the last of our libations and poring over the map at Elk Meadows. Wait a minute. What's this? The trail down from Elk Meadows itself crosses Newton Creek a thousand feet below the spot where we turned back? What's that green line on the other side of the creek? Another trail that climbs back up the mountain and intersects with—no, it couldn't be—the Timberline Trail?

My countenance brightens immediately. If we hit this lower Newton Creek crossing at first light tomorrow morning, before the ice and snow high above get a chance to warm and melt, we have a good shot at making it across. And then it's just two miles back up to the Timberline Trail and seven and a half to the lodge. It all starts to click. Glory and trumpets.

Except that Amy's aching hip and blisters are not on board. Instead, she's at least game to hike back up to the Timberline Trail and over to Mt. Hood Meadows, but from there she'll bow out gracefully and wait for me and Oliver to knock off the remaining four and a half miles, pick up the car, and head back to get her. A noble gesture on her part, but it is a downer to realize that after all this, she's not going to make it.

Still, that night I fall to sleep with, I swear, a smile on my face.

THE FINAL MORNING DAWNS *as beautiful as can be, but we don't tarry. It's rise and shine, pack up, and grab a bite on the trail. There's tension in the air from the get-go, and it builds as the shushing of Newton Creek amps up through the trees. Maybe we're already too late. Maybe I'll be thumbing that ride after all.*

But the creek down here this morning turns out to be tame and sleepy. Shallow riffles are all that skim down through the rocks, and we ford our way across as if splashing through puddles in a crosswalk. And there, just as the map promised, is the spur trail heading back up the south side of the creek toward the Timberline Trail. We are back on track.

The mood lightens immediately, and in no time at all we're winding along, stepping over Clark Creek, and wending in and out of the grassy, treed slopes and crystalline streams that mark the edge of the Mt. Hood Meadows ski area. Soon we're passing under idle ski lifts and approaching a gravel road that I'm thinking will be Amy's bail-out point. We get to the road, though, and she just keeps trucking. I catch a grin on her face when she turns around as we push away from Meadows. She's going the rest of the way.

To say Amy's got a renewed spring in her step hardly covers it. She's powering her way through the tall trees beyond Meadows and dropping us down into the White River basin at a pace that pounds my knees and sets me up for some pleasant tendonitis once we get back into the city. Just before we break out of the trees into the wide-open expanse of the basin, we pass a foreboding sign. I don't remember its exact words, but it was something about danger, death, and the White River's notorious debris flows that barrel down the mountain.

Amy again has tears in her eyes when I catch up to her at river's edge. What now? I'm thinking. But it turns out to be more relief than anything else, because right now, there's a safe and obvious crossing before us. Our last one.

Over the silty gray river we go, up the other side, across a few ashen plains. Hood is glorious from here, towering up into an untouched blue sky. The last two and a half miles of the trail head up through a dark stand of Douglas firs and then snake along *wide-open grassy hillsides. Up ahead, Timberline Lodge taunts like an oasis as Oliver begins to slow. The poor hound is hot. His tongue lolls long, his black coat absorbing the direct rays of the sun like asphalt. My water becomes his, and damn if the dog doesn't finally figure out the beauty of shade, thirty-nine miles into the trail. He takes five under ever tree, every shrub, every sliver of cover he can find, and we let him. We're not losing anybody at this point.*

Then it's down and up one final gully, over a last hump, through one more clumsy stumble, to the bustling pavement at Timberline Lodge.

We are done.

AFTERWORD

The past is the ink with which we write the present.

—Breyten Breytenbach, "The Faces of Ants"

After eight years of exploring Mount Hood, climbing it, camping around it, paddling the lakes at its base, eating apples and pears and drinking wine born of the volcano's soil and water, I felt like I knew the mountain pretty well. But something about ticking off the Timberline Trail made me look at Mount Hood in a different way. Now when I saw McNeil Point from afar, I knew exactly where Ramona Falls was in relation and where the cut-through on Bald Mountain should be. I knew for the first time about Gnarl Ridge and Newton Creek, what it's like to hike through Mt. Hood Meadows in the summer, and that there are waterfalls and campsites and gigantic Douglas firs all over the mountain that most people will never see. Amy and I both consider that trip a highlight of all our time on the mountain. So far, anyway.

A couple weeks after we'd finished the Timberline Trail, a feat we'd celebrated with a dip in Trillium Lake and giant burgers and beers at Calamity Jane's, a homey hamburger joint in Sandy, Tchaikovsky came calling.

Every year, the Oregon Symphony ends its summer music season with a glorious concert at Tom McCall Waterfront Park on the Willamette River in downtown Portland. It's always the Thursday before Labor Day, and if there's a better time to guarantee ideal weather in Oregon, I've not yet found it. The days are warm, the nights just hinting at autumn cool. Daylight slips into sunset in the early evening, coloring the mountain off on the eastern horizon a hazy blend of gray and white, pink and orange. The evening of the concert, revelers gather by the thousands on the green park lawn to sip wine and capture the last moments of summer. The final number of the night, once the sky has gone black, the mountain's disappeared, and the sailboats have pulled in close to hear the music, is always the *1812 Overture*, replete with cannons and fireworks.

It is by far one of my favorite events of the year in Portland.

We went to the 2005 concert and celebrated the ending of summer that night in rare form. Nine months later, we welcomed our daughter, Madeline, into the world.

A year and a half after Madeline joined us, a pack bigger than I'd ever seen and heavier than I'd ever carried—and that was even before I added twenty pounds of toddler to it—leaned up against the car. We were parked on the road into Mt. Hood Meadows near the Umbrella Falls trail on Hood's east side, dead set on notching at least one backpacking trip that summer. I lifted Madeline into the pack and heaved the whole lot onto my back, wobbling at first under the awkward weight. She smiled and laughed and promptly set about drinking all my water as we headed up the trail.

We didn't go too far that first trip, just a couple miles up above the Timberline Trail to a flat tent spot among the ash and blown-down trees left over from the mountain's last outburst two centuries earlier. Under a beautiful blue sky, Madeline sifted gray ash through her hands like sand on the beach and called out *mow mow* every time she caught Hood's enormous visage in the background. That night, whipping winds slapped and bowed the tent walls. When they hadn't relented by early the next morning, we decided to skip breakfast on the mountain and head down. Not an ideal exit—we'd envisioned a lazy morning of sunshine on the hill—but for Madeline, a great introduction to Mount Hood and its backcountry beauty all the same.

Since then, we've been back to the mountain with her more times than I can remember. We once camped for a night at the relatively unheard-of Owl Point and watched a helicopter and its bucket drift back and forth between Laurence Lake and a growing plume of smoke rising from the forest up near Cooper Spur. We broke in a new sled at the White River Sno-Park on one absolutely perfect day in February. She's been to Timberline Lodge so many times that she knows exactly where to find Bruno, the lodge's resident Saint Bernard. Madeline's also pulled newts from Trillium Lake with Hood high up as backdrop, hung out with us for a day of climbing at Frenches Dome on the mountain's western base, and spent countless camping nights exhausted and fighting sleep to the sound of the Muddy Fork nearby.

In the spring of 2010 somebody else started joining us on the mountain, too: Madeline's brother, Spencer. He was just three weeks old when we all went up to visit a friend in a snowy Steiner cabin in Government Camp, and just six months the first time he spent a sunny, mountain-filled weekend at a favorite Muddy Fork campsite with Hood bright and soaring above the river.

I'm sure as long as we're here and it's here, we'll all keep going back to Mount Hood. Its wild beauty, its history, its refuge, its excitement—everything about the mountain is part of why I came out here and why I've stayed. Maybe someday soon Madeline and Spencer will learn how to ski up there. Maybe someday we'll all tackle the Timberline Trail again. Maybe someday we'll even climb it together.

Whatever happens, Mount Hood is already a big part of their lives. To them, it's just natural and always will be. To me, there's simply nothing better.

BIBLIOGRAPHY

Ambach, W., E. Ambach, W. Tributsch, R. Henn, and H. Unterdorfer. "Corpses Released from Glacier Ice: Glaciological and Forensic Aspects." *Journal of Wilderness Medicine* 3, no. 4 (November 1992): 372–376.

Arthur, Jean. *Timberline and a Century of Skiing on Mount Hood.* Whitefish, MT: Whitefish Editions, 1998.

Barcott, Bruce. *The Measure of a Mountain: Beauty and Terror on Mount Rainier.* Seattle: Sasquatch Books, 1997.

Beckey, Fred. *Challenge of the North Cascades.* Seattle: The Mountaineers Books, 1969 and 1996.

Burroughs, William J., Bob Crowder, Ted Robertson, Eleanor Vallier-Talbot, and Richard Whitaker. *Weather.* McMahons Point, New South Wales, Australia: 1996.

Cameron, Kenneth A., and Patrick T. Pringle. "Prehistoric buried forests of Mount Hood." *Oregon Geology* 53, no. 2 (March 1991): 34–43.

Cohen, David Elliot, and Rick Smolan. *Oregon 24/7.* New York: DK Publishing, Inc., 2004.

Dresbeck, Rachel. *Oregon Disasters: True Stories of Tragedy and Survival.* Guilford, CT: The Globe Pequot Press, Insiders' Guide, 2006.

Driedger, Carolyn L., and Paul M. Kennard. "Ice Volumes on Cascade Volcanoes: Mount Rainier, Mount Hood, and Mount Shasta." *U. S. Geological Survey Professional Paper 1365,* 1986.

Durbin, Kathie. *Tree Huggers: Victory, Defeat & Renewal in the Northwest Ancient Forest Campaign.* Seattle: The Mountaineers Books, 1996.

Egan, Timothy. *The Good Rain: Across Time and Terrain in the Pacific Northwest.* New York: Alfred A. Knopf, Inc., 1990.

Ellinger, Jonathan R. "The Changing Glaciers of Mt. Hood, Oregon and Mt. Rainier, Washington: Implications for Periglacial Debris Flows." Master's thesis, Oregon State University, 2010.

Fortner, Sarah K. "The Geochemistry of Glacier Snow and Melt: The Oregon Cascades and the Taylor Valley, Antartica." PhD dissertation, Ohio State University, 2008.

Grauer, Jack. *Mount Hood: A Complete History*. 8th ed. Vancouver, WA: Jack Grauer, 2010.

Harmon, Rick. "Oregon Places: The Bull Run Watershed: Portland's Enduring Jewel," *Oregon Historical Quarterly* 96 (Summer-Fall, 1995): 242–270.

Harris, Stephen L. *Fire Mountains of the West: The Cascade and Mono Lake Volcanoes*. 3rd ed. Missoula, MT: Mountain Press Publishing Company, 2005.

Hatton, Raymond R., and George H. Taylor. *The Oregon Weather Book: A State of Extremes*. Corvallis: Oregon State University Press, 1999.

Henderson, George. *Lonely on the Mountain: A Skier's Memoir*. Victoria, BC: Trafford Publishing, 2006.

Holaday, Ann. *The Mountain Never Cries: A Mother's Diary*. Wilsonville, OR: Book Partners, 1999.

Hood River County Historical Society, friends, and families. *History of Hood River County, Oregon 1852–1982*. Hood River, OR: Hood River County Historical Society, 1982.

Hurd, Kathryn. *The Dwyers: Pioneers in the Timber Industry*. Estacada, OR: Meripah Press, 2004.

Jackson, Keith M., and Andrew G. Fountain. "Spatial and Morphological Change on Eliot Glacier, Mount Hood, Oregon, USA." *Annals of Glaciology* 46, no. 1 (October 2007): 222–226.

Kerr, Andy. *Oregon Wild: Endangered Forest Wilderness*. Portland: Oregon Natural Resources Council, 2004.

LaMarca, Christopher. *Forest Defenders: The Confrontational American Landscape*. New York: powerHouse Books, 2008.

LeMonds, James. *Deadfall: Generations of Logging in the Pacific Northwest*. Missoula, MT: Mountain Press Publishing Company, 2001.

Lichen, Patricia K. *River-Walking Songbirds & Singing Coyotes: An Uncommon Field Guide to Northwest Mountains*. Seattle: Sasquatch Books, 2001.

Lillquist, Karl, and Karen Walker. "Historical Glacier and Climate Fluctuations at Mount Hood, Oregon." *Arctic, Antarctic, and Alpine Research* 38, no. 3 (2006): 399–412.

Lorain, Douglas. *Afoot & Afield Portland/Vancouver: A comprehensive hiking guide.* 2nd ed. Berkley, CA: Wilderness Press, 2008.

Lorain, Douglas. *Backpacking Oregon.* Berkley, CA: Wilderness Press, 1999.

Mass, Cliff. *The Weather of the Pacific Northwest.* Seattle: University of Washington Press, 2008.

Mathews, Daniel. *Cascade-Olympic Natural History: A Trailside Reference.* 2nd ed. Portland, OR: Raven Editions, 1999.

McArthur, Lewis A., and Lewis L. McArthur. *Oregon Geographic Names.* 7th ed. Portland: Oregon Historical Society Press, 2003.

McNeil, Fred H. *McNeil's Mount Hood: Wy'East the Mountain Revisited.* Edited by Joseph A. Stein. Zigzag, OR: The Zig Zag Papers, 1990.

Miller, Joesph, et al. *Bull Run: A World Treasure.* Portland, OR: Bull Run Interest Group, 1998.

Morris Bishop, Ellen. *In Search of Ancient Oregon.* Portland, OR: Timber Press, Inc., 2003.

Munro, Sarah Baker. *Timberline Lodge: The History, Art, and Craft of an American Icon.* Portland, OR: Timber Press, Inc., 2009.

Nehring, Nancy L., Harold A. Wollenberg, and David A. Johnston. "Gas Analyses of Fumaroles from Mt. Hood, Oregon." U.S. Geological Survey Open-File Report 81-236, Menlo Park, CA: 1980.

Nelson, Jim, and Peter Potterfield. *Selected Climbs in the Cascades: Volume I.* 2nd ed. Seattle: The Mountaineers Books, 2003.

Nesbit, Sharon, "Dr. Miller Remembered for Battles to Save Bull Run," *The Gresham Outlook.* July 2, 2007.

Nolin, Anne W., Jeff Phillipe, Anne Jefferson, and Sarah L. Lewis. "Present-Day and Future Contributions of Glacier Runoff to Summertime Flows in a Pacific Northwest Watershed: Implications for Water Resources." *Water Resources Journal,* in press, 2010.

Orr, Elizabeth L., and William N. Orr. *Geology of Oregon*. 5th ed. Dubuque, IA: Kendall/Hunt Publishing Company, 2000.

Price, Larry W. *Biogeography Field Guide to Cascade Mountains: Transect along U.S. Highway 26 in Oregon*. Portland: Portland State University, Department of Geography: 1971.

Renner, Jeff. *Mountain Weather: Backcountry Forecasting and Weather Safety for Hikers, Campers, Climbers, Skiers, and Snowboarders*. Seattle: The Mountaineers Books, 2005.

Roberts, Rad, "Climber 9-1-1: Should mobile communication devices be mandatory?" *Northwest Mountaineering Journal* 7 (Summer 2010).

Rose, Judith, ed. *Timberline Lodge: A Love Story*. Portland, OR: Friends of Timberline and Graphic Arts Center Publishing Company, 1986.

Sheehan, Madelynne Diness. *Fishing in Oregon: Where and When to Go, What to Bring, How to Get There, and What You'll Find*. 9th ed. Scappoose, OR: Flying Pencil Publications, 2000.

Twight, Mark. *Kiss or Kill: Confessions of a Serial Climber*. Seattle: The Mountaineers Books, 2001.

Van Tilburg, Christopher. *Mountain Rescue Doctor: Wilderness Medicine in the Extremes of Nature*. New York: St. Martin's Press, 2007.

Whitney, Stephen R., and Rob Sandelin. *Field Guide to the Cascades & Olympics*. 2nd ed. Seattle: The Mountaineers Books, 2003.

Wood, Charles Arthur. *Volcanoes of North America: United States and Canada*. Cambridge: Cambridge University Press, 1992.

Wood, Wendell. *A Walking Guide to Oregon's Ancient Forests*. Portland: Oregon Natural Resources Council, 1991.

Writers' Program of the Work Projects Administration. *Mount Hood: A Guide*. New York: Duell, Sloan and Pearce, 1940.

ACKNOWLEDGMENTS

I WOULD LIKE TO EXTEND my sincere gratitude to all the people who shared their stories and reverence for Mount Hood with me throughout this entire book. It is a long list that includes not only every name already mentioned in these pages, but many others who helped along the way. A hearty thank-you and an apology as well for anyone I may have missed.

Thankfully, Susan Roxborough had been thinking about publishing a Mount Hood book when my proposal landed on her desk at Sasquatch Books. The great team at Sasquatch, both staff and freelance, also included publisher Gary Luke, Kurt Stephan, Michael Townley, Anna Goldstein, Shari Miranda, and Liza Brice-Dahmen. Doug Lorain walked me through the author process, and his indispensable backpacking guide helped Amy and me walk all the way around Mount Hood. Bruce Barcott shared his advice and also wrote the mountain book that inspired mine. It was an honor to meet Jack Grauer, who has been telling the Mount Hood story for more than thirty-five years in his classic *Mount Hood: A Complete History*. The Mazamas let me pore over their library and crash their Friday night glacier show. Willie Scott was a wealth of geological knowledge. Thanks also to Randy Nickelsen Clark, Mary Jo Cohen, Guy and Chiyoko Meacham, Marshall Gannett, Dennis and Deena Kraft, Joe Keating, Gary Larsen, Steve McCarthy, Harry Oakes, Jim Rice, Chuck Thomsen, and Dave Tragethon.

My parents taught me to love books and have always been there. Oliver kept me company on the trail and late at night in my office. Madeline called it Mountain Hood, making me smile,

Spencer said my name for the first time the day I finished the first draft, and Amy explored the mountain with me—and then let me write about it.

INDEX

ABOUT THE AUTHOR

JON BELL grew up in Ohio but he has been writing in Oregon since 1997. His work has appeared in numerous publications, including the *Oregonian, Backpacker,* and *Oregon Coast.* He lives with his wife, two kids, and a black Lab in Lake Oswego, Oregon.